—African-American Biographies—

COLIN POWELL

Soldier and Patriot

Series Consultant:
Dr. Russell L. Adams, Chairman
Department of Afro-American Studies, Howard University

Anne Schraff

Enslow Publishers, Inc.

44 Fadem Road	PO Box 38
Box 699	Aldershot
Springfield, NJ 07081	Hants GU12 6BP
USA	UK

MLK 443-1021

Library of Congress Cataloging-in-Publication Data

Schraff, Anne E.
    Colin Powell: soldier and patriot / Anne Schraff.
    p. cm. —(African-American biographies)
    Includes bibliographical references and index.
    Summary: Surveys the life and career of Colin Powell, from his
childhood in the South Bronx, through his years of military service, to
his work in the United States government.
    ISBN 0-89490-810-3
    1. Powell, Colin L.—Juvenile literature. 2. Generals—United States—
Biography—Juvenile literature. 3. Afro-American generals—Biography—
Juvenile literature. 4. United States. Army—Biography—Juvenile
literature. [1. Powell, Colin L. 2. Generals. 3. Afro-Americans—
Biography.] I.Title. II. Series.
E840.5.P68S35   1997
355'.0092—dc20
[B]
                                                96-19974
                                                   CIP
                                                   AC
Printed in the United States of America

10 9 8 7 6 5 4 3 2

Illustration Credits:
City College of the City University of New York, p. 25; Courtesy of
General Colin Powell, pp. 12, 15, 17, 22, 35, 36, 41, 54; Department of
Defense, pp. 4, 91, 95, 98, 100, 104, 115; United States Army, Fort Carson,
Colorado, p. 59; United States Army, Fort Leavenworth, pp. 63, 64.

Cover Illustration:
Courtesy of General Colin Powell

CONTENTS

Colin Powell

1

"OUR VALOR WAS NEVER IN QUESTION"

he thirty-one-year-old African-American officer, Major Colin Powell, was on his second tour of duty in Vietnam. The year was 1968, an agonizing time in American history. In April, civil rights activist Martin Luther King, Jr., had been killed by a sniper in Memphis, Tennessee. In June, presidential candidate Senator Robert Kennedy of New York had been slain in Los Angeles, California. All the while, the war in Vietnam raged with ever greater fury. During Tet, the Vietnamese New Year, the North Vietnamese and their southern sympathizers, the Viet Cong, had attacked cities and military targets all over South Vietnam. Riots and protests swept American cities.

Now, on this November day in 1968, in a region west of the village of Quang Ngai, Division Commander Charles Gettys, Colonel Jack Treadwell, two aides, and a crew of four rode in a Huey helicopter along with Major Colin Powell, the operations officer. They were about to inspect a captured enemy camp in the jungle. The Viet Cong had used it to harass Americans with sniper fire, mines, and booby traps.

A red smoke flare guided Pilot Warrant Officer James Hannan to a small landing zone. Hannan's first attempt to land was unsuccessful, so he flew off and tried again more slowly from the north. Gunner Bob Pyle called out that it was clear on the right. The crew chief said it looked clear on the left.

Major Powell watched from a side window as the helicopter lowered. Branches were slashed by the rotor blade, and leaves swirled in the air. Suddenly the rotor blade caught a tree trunk about six inches around. The helicopter tilted left and began a straight plunge down to the ground of fifty to one hundred feet. Aware of the impending crash, Powell prepared. He later recalled, "I bent over, put my hands under my knees, and waited for it to hit."[1]

As the helicopter crash-landed in the jungle, its structure crumpled and caved in on some of the men. Powell suffered a broken ankle, but he was able to push open his door and escape. The engine whined shrilly, and smoke began to rise. There was great danger of a spark igniting the ruptured fuel tank.

"Get away, get away, it's gonna explode," Powell shouted.[2] Gunner Pyle escaped behind him. Still inside the shattered helicopter were Gettys, Treadwell, and the others. Some were badly injured, and some were trapped. In the event of an explosion they would all be killed.

The pilot's door was jammed by the crash, and he was also pinned in the wreck by an armrest. Powell struggled to pull a nearly unconscious Gettys to safety while Pyle tried to free the pilot. With Gettys safely away from the crash, Powell returned for the others. He next helped rescue Treadwell, who was unconscious with head lacerations.

Powell returned to the smoking and dangerous wreck a third time for Ron Tumelson, the general's aide. Tumelson's head was trapped between a radio console and the engine, which had smashed through the fuselage. Powell later recalled, "Tumelson was covered with blood. I saw no sign of life and was sure he was dead. I managed to shove aside the dislodged console and free him. And then I heard him groan."[3] Tumelson did survive and was walking several days later.

Powell remained at the scene, helping the last of the crew members to safety. He later said of his actions that day, "I wasn't alone. It wasn't anything heroic."[4] He was

awarded the Soldier's Medal for bravery in a
noncombat incident where he had voluntarily risked his
own life. The young officer had already won the Purple
Heart and Bronze Star on the battlefields of Vietnam.

Years after his Vietnam service, General Colin
Powell stood at the Vietnam Veterans Memorial in
Washington, D.C., and said of those who served with
him, "I owed them my total loyalty."[5]

On Memorial Day, 1991, General Powell had these
words for the assembled veterans and all Americans:

> You need no redemption. You redeemed yourself at
> Hue. You redeemed yourself in the A Shau Valley. You
> redeemed yourself at Dau Tieng, at Khe Sanh, in the
> South China Sea, in the air over Hanoi, or launching
> off Yankee Station, and in a thousand other places.
> The parades and celebrations are not needed to
> restore our honor as Vietnam veterans because we
> never lost our honor. They're not to clear up the matter
> of our valor because our valor was never in question.[6]

Commenting on the career of Colin Powell, an old
friend, Harlan Ullman, wondered aloud: "Where did
it come from? You have a black kid who was born poor
in the Bronx, who goes through City College, and all
of a sudden you have this extraordinary persona—
where did it come from? How did he get it?"[7]

A large part of the answer lies in the family and
strong traditions from which this man came.

2

HARLEM, HUNT'S POINT, AND KELLY STREET

"My parents were hard-working people," Colin Powell said. "My father was gone all day, every day. He never came home before seven or eight at night. My mother came home tired, too."[1]

Luther Theophilus Powell, Colin Powell's father, was a small man about five feet two inches tall. He came to America on a banana boat, the first of his Jamaican family to emigrate. He went directly to Harlem where about one hundred and fifty thousand Jamaicans already lived at that time. The Powells had been peasant farmers in Jamaica. Powell said of his father, "He was a patriarch because of his wisdom, because of his willingness to help anybody who needed help. He loved people. He would do anything to help them."[2] Powell referred to his father as "the formative figure in my life."[3]

Maud Ariel McKoy, Powell's mother, also came from Jamaica to Harlem in the 1920s. Unlike Luther Powell, who had to quit school as a boy, Maud McKoy was a high school graduate. She was the disciplinarian in the family.[4] "She could cut me down with a single glance," Powell recalled.[5]

The young immigrants met at a picnic in Pelham Bay Park, a favorite summer spot. They were married on December 28, 1929, at St. Philip's Church in Harlem. Both Powells worked in New York's garment district. Powell's mother did piecework, putting buttons and trim on women's clothing. She kept a tag for each garment she worked on. She wrapped the tags in bundles held by rubber bands and presented them weekly to get her pay. Powell's father worked in a warehouse and then became foreman of the shipping department of Ginsburg's, a manufacturer of women's clothing.

In 1931, the Powell's first child, Marilyn, was born. On April 5, 1937, Colin Luther Powell was born. Soon after Colin's birth, the Powells moved from Harlem to Hunt's Point in the South Bronx. It was a lower-middle-class working neighborhood. The Powells lived among neighbors who were Jewish, Italian, Irish, and Greek. Puerto Rican immigrants joined them during the 1940s.

In 1943, while Colin was still a small boy, the family moved to 952 Kelly Street, between Westchester Avenue and 163rd Street, where many cousins also lived. It was here that Colin spent the happiest days of his childhood.

"What many people now call a slum was a tenement neighborhood and a neat place to grow up when I was a boy," Powell later recalled.[6] The Powells lived on the third floor of an eight-family, four-story building, now demolished. Powell's sister remembers, "It was sort of like living in a small town. Each neighborhood had its own character."[7]

Young Colin played thirty-six kinds of street games, including stickball, stoopball, punchball, and sluggo.[8] Checkers was also popular, with Colin and his friends pouring hot wax into cola bottle caps to make their own game pieces. Sometimes the children flew kites with razor tails from the roofs.

Powell's favorite childhood pastime was "making the walk," a counter-clockwise walk around the area.[9] He passed Jewish bakeries and candy stores, a Puerto Rican grocery store, and countless butcher shops. Every nationality, including Jamaicans, had a specialty store. The pungent smells of cheese wedges and salamis filled the air.

"Our Saturday-morning rite was to go to the

Young Colin Powell, shown here at age seven or eight, spent the happiest days of his childhood on Kelly Street.

Tiffany Theatre and watch the serial and then a double feature of cowboy movies," Powell remembers.[10]

"Everybody was a 'minority'," Powell recalls, "I did not know what a 'majority' was. You were either black, Puerto Rican, Jewish, or of some strange European extraction."[11]

The Powell house was a center of hospitality. Powell's father enjoyed inviting everyone in to share food and drink.

Children in the neighborhood with two-wheel bikes felt important, and for just a nickel, they could use the trolley or subway to travel all over New York. Colin attended Public School 39 at Kelly and Longwood streets. When he was nine, he found himself in the bottom group of fourth grade. "My sister was already an excellent student, destined for college," Powell recalls, "and here I was, having difficulty in fourth grade."[12]

In 1949, Colin attended Junior High School 52, just up the street from home. It was an all-boys school. Colin's close friend, Gene Norman, recalls it as "a little bit of a tough place."[13] Another classmate called it "a dangerous place, a very tough place." He remembers: "Fights in the halls, teachers got pushed against the wall. The shop teachers used to run around with boards to fend off the aggressors. The principal, it is more than rumored, walked around with a pistol."[14]

In September 1950, Colin Powell entered Morris High School. There he studied college preparatory courses and took part in track, winning a letter.

As Colin was entering his teens, the neighborhood was changing for the worse. In 1991, General Powell returned to Morris High to recall his school days. At that time, he said:

> We had lots of drugs in my neighborhood. On every street corner was some pothead or junkie trying to sell or deal or get others involved in it. I didn't do it. Never in my life, not even to experiment. Not even to try, not to see what it would be like.[15]

He went on to recall how many of his Morris High classmates ended up dead or in jail. Explaining his own success, he said, "I credit most of that to my family, to a very close family, a family that had expectations for the children of that family."[16] Powell told the students that taking drugs was "the most self-destructive thing you could do with the life that God and your parents had given you.[17]

As a teenager, Colin held many jobs, but the most influential one was at Sickser's baby furniture store. Colin was on his way to the post office to buy stamps for his mother when a white-haired man stepped from a store to ask him if he wanted to earn some money. The man was Jay Sickser, and he was so impressed with Colin's skills in unloading a truck filled with merchandise that he hired the youth to work daily after

Colin Powell (second from right) entered Morris High School in 1950. Here he is shown with friends from Kelly Street.

school. Colin assembled furniture, boxed shipments, and set up displays. Colin put in twelve to fifteen hours a week for fifty to seventy-five cents an hour. The hard working boy was always on time and friendly to the customers, and he kept this job into his college years.

Growing up, Colin was surrounded by a large extended family of aunts, uncles, and cousins. His relatives passed on their rich culture to the younger members. Holidays were festive times with multicourse meals of turkey, ham, peas, sweet potatoes, and special Jamaican rum cakes. The Powells were deeply religious Episcopalians (a Protestant denomination) and Colin was an altar-server at St. Margaret's Church.

Colin had heard so much about Jamaica that he could not wait to see it for himself. As a young man, he went there and saw all the landmarks his family had told him about. In a 1990 interview, Powell talked about his culture: "Most West Indians are high Anglicans, the same as high Episcopalians—the higher the better. Their value system is a combination of the family and the British tradition."[18]

Colin Powell's cousin, successful businessperson Bruce Llewellyn, compared the different attitudes of Jamaican immigrants and southern African-Americans this way. "We tended to see it differently from southern blacks. They saw the glass as mostly empty. We saw it as half full, and we were coming to fill up the rest."[19]

Colin's parents urged their children to get a good

Colin Powell along with his parents, Maud and Luther Powell, attended sister Marilyn's graduation from Buffalo State College in 1952.

education. Although sister Marilyn was always an excellent student, Colin admits that he did not take school seriously. He recalls that his youthful dreams were small as he walked the halls of Morris High. He simply wanted to get out of New York, have a job, and get some excitement.[20]

In June 1954, after three and one-half years of high school, Colin graduated. Two years earlier his sister, Marilyn, had graduated from Buffalo State College.

It was expected that the sixteen-year-old Colin would go to college. "I went to college for a single reason," he admitted. "My parents expected it."[21] Colin's mother urged her son to go into engineering because "that's where the money is."[22] Since Colin had no special career interests of his own, that is the direction he went.

Colin Powell recalled his first day of college: "As I took in the grand gothic structures, a C-average student out of middling Morris High School, I felt overwhelmed."[23]

Colin had been accepted to two colleges, City College of New York and New York University. City College had an annual tuition of $10. New York University asked for tuition of $750 a year. The choice was easy. The Powells had little money to spare. The tall teenager would live at home where it was cheaper. He would commute to college, a place he was not yet sure he even belonged.

3

PERSHING RIFLES TO FULDA GAP

olin Powell enrolled as an engineering student, but he found he did not like the subject. His grades averaged a *B* in the first semester of a very hard schedule. The following summer he took a class in mechanical drawing. One day the teacher asked the students to draw a plane intersecting a cone in space. Other students began drawing, but Powell thought, "For the life of me, I could not visualize a plane intersecting a cone in space. If this was engineering, the game was over."[1] It was the turning point for the freshman. He knew he just was not cut out for engineering. But what was he good at? Powell switched his major to geology. The trouble was he did not like geology much either. He asked himself, "What did you do with geology? Where did you go with it? Prospecting for oil? A novel pursuit for a black kid from the South Bronx."[2]

While in college, Powell got a job at the Coca-Cola bottling plant. He was hired to mop floors. Looking back on the experience, he explained:

> . . . and black kids, well, of course you got to mop the floors, and white kids worked on the bottling machines. And so I mopped floors. The heck with it—ninety cents an hour. And I learned how to mop. When somebody comes and dumps about fifty cases of cola on the floor, I want to tell you, that is some serious mopping.[3]

The foreman was pleased with Powell's work and attitude, and he promoted Powell the following summer. Powell joined the white boys at the bottling machine. Later he became the inspector and finally the deputy foreman on the machine. The experience shows how Powell generally dealt with racial discrimination. He refused to be bitter, and with stubborn determination, he simply proved himself.

As he worked toward a geology degree, Powell still was not enjoying college. He discovered that he was not very "good at physics, calculus, geology, history, languages, or any of the other [courses]."[4]

Yet there was something going on at City College that did appeal to Powell. He was attracted to something unusual on a college campus like CCNY with its liberal traditions. "Young guys on campus in uniforms" was what caught Powell's eye.[5] What Powell saw was the Army Reserve Officers Training Corps (ROTC) and specifically the Pershing Rifles, a military society that acted as a drill team.

Powell joined up and was given his olive-drab pants and jacket, brown shirt, brown tie, brown shoes, a belt with a brass buckle, and an overseas cap [a woolen cap without a visor]. When he got home, he put on his uniform and looked in the mirror. "The uniform gave me a sense of belonging," he recalled, "and something I had never experienced all the while I was growing up; I felt distinctive."[6]

One Pershing Rifle member was a young black man, Ronald Brooks, two years older than Powell. Brooks was a cadet leader in the ROTC and an officer in the Pershing Rifles. He appeared to have all the qualities that Powell felt lacking in himself. "I had found a model and a mentor. I set out to remake myself in the Ronnie Brooks mold," Powell remembers.[7]

Powell had been on sports teams in high school and even spent some time in the Boy Scouts, but these did not produce the sense of belonging he found in the Pershing Rifles.[8] Powell learned map-reading, drill and ceremonies, basic infantry tactics, army procedures, and rife marksmanship. During the summer, he went away to camp for field experiences.

Colin Powell relaxes in a hammock while at ROTC summer camp in 1957.

The members of the Pershing Rifles were of many different ethnic backgrounds. Race, color, and financial background meant nothing here. The young men drilled together and partied together. They stood up for one another like brothers. Powell thought, "If this was what soldiering was all about, then maybe I wanted to be a soldier."[9]

Soon the activities of the Pershing Rifles were dominating Powell's life. "I spent the next four years concentrating on ROTC, spending most of my time on Pershing Rifles activities and tolerating the academic demands of the college as best I could," he said.[10]

During Powell's junior year, he started the ROTC advanced program. His duties included recruiting for the Pershing Rifles. He enjoyed this task very much. He had such enthusiasm for the program that it was easy to convey his excitement to new recruits. Powell recruited twenty-one new members, including a Greek-American student named Tony Mavroudis. Mavroudis became a protégé and dear friend. Powell said he loved Mavroudis "like a brother."[11] Powell and Mavroudis spent time together, double-dated, lived in each other's homes, and called each other's parents "Mom and Dad."[12]

In June 1958, Powell graduated from college with barely a *C* grade average. He received his bachelor's degree in geology. He said he did it by "mastering the rock formations under Manhattan."[13] What really mattered to him was how well he had done in ROTC— straight *A*'s.

On June 9, 1958, Powell entered CCNY's Aronowitz Auditorium with the First Army Band playing. A few weeks before, his father had given him the money to buy a uniform from the best military haberdasher in New York. Wearing his brand new uniform, Powell repeated with his classmates, "I, Colin Luther Powell, do solemnly swear that I will support and defend the Constitution of the United States against all enemies foreign and domestic." Powell recalled that even four decades later the memory of that night "sent a shiver down my spine."[14]

Powell was named the Distinguished Military Graduate of his group. This proved very important. As a graduate of West Point, Powell would have received a regular Army Commission and become a second lieutenant in the Army. Instead, as an ROTC graduate, he was commissioned a second lieutenant in the Army Reserve. Because of his position as Distinguished Military Graduate, he only had to be a reserve officer for one month. On June 30, 1958, he became a proud second lieutenant in the United States Army.

Now Powell was in the Army, and he had to take basic training. He said goodbye to his parents, who now owned their own home on Elmira Avenue in

Colin Powell received his bachelor's degree in geology in 1958.

Queens, New York, and he boarded a bus for Georgia. At this point, his parents did not think he was making the Army his career. They expected he would act as most young men did by serving his three years of military duty and then coming home to a real job.

Powell arrived at Fort Benning, Georgia, and a whole new world for him. He never had lived in the South before, and he never had seen segregation in practice. He found he could shop at the dime store in Columbus, Georgia, but he could not eat at their lunch counter. He could buy at a department store, but he could not use the men's room. A white corporal drove him to a black church in Gainesville, Georgia, on Sunday, but the corporal was advised that he could not enter the church with Powell.

Powell began five months of military training at Fort Benning, the home of the Infantry School and a training ground for infantry and airborne troops. Many of America's top generals began their careers as infantrymen.

The Infantry Officer Basic Course (IOBC) was held in a cluster of cinder-block buildings at Fort Benning. The young soldiers reviewed all they had learned in college, as well as new subjects. Powell found the class work and weapons training easy. The infantry usually fights on foot, so Powell and his comrades learned hand-to-hand combat. They learned the use of weapons like rifles, pistols, machine guns, grenades, mortars, and flamethrowers.

The field course was a real challenge for a city youth like Powell, who was accustomed to the orderly layout of New York's city streets. One assignment was to hike five miles at night, guided by a compass, to find a stake planted in the Georgia wilderness. The obstacle course was brutal, but it had to be overcome to complete outdoor field training. In the hot, humid climate of Georgia, many of the trainees became heat casualties. When everyone else seemed to be falling victim to the weather, Powell cracked a joke or managed a grin.[15] It looked like Powell was born to be a soldier.

After finishing basic training, Powell requested both ranger and airborne schools. After completing both, he would be capable of serving in any capacity as an infantryman. He wanted a complete background so he would be ready for any combat situation.

The three-week airborne course at Fort Benning included hard physical training. There were repetitive exercises such as running and push-ups. The young soldiers had to appear before dawn for inspection in spit-shined boots. The future paratroopers were preparing for a demanding task—jumping from an airplane, hitting the dirt, and being ready to fight. There were practice parachute landings, falls, exits from mock doors, and jumping from thirty-foot-high practice towers. Finally the young paratroopers were dropped from a two-hundred-and-fifty-foot-high gondola. Then, at last, there was real parachuting. Colin Powell learned how to jump from a plane, land safely, and be a combat-ready infantryman. He earned his jump wings and became "jump qualified."

Ranger school is the ultimate infantry soldier's proving ground. For two weeks, they experience the worst conditions that might be met on the battlefield. At the Fort Benning school, Powell and the others marched through mud, sweating and exhausted. During long-range night marches through the Georgia swamps, the men met snakes and snapping turtles. They were weighed down with fifty-pound field sacks. They carried a rifle or machine gun over their shoulders and wore heavy steel helmets. Through it all, Second Lieutenant Powell kept his sense of humor and his confidence.

While at Fort Benning, Powell joined the Officers Club, which offered a dining room, lounge, tennis court, and pool. This provided a welcome social respite from the segregated situation beyond the camp. Powell fit in well and enjoyed the company of the other officers. Powell earned $222.30 a month plus housing allowance.

In January 1958, Powell finished training. He was ready to be a soldier in the field. His first assignment was to help man an outpost during the Cold War with the Soviet Union. Powell arrived in Germany in October 1958. He was stationed at the Fulda Gap in West Germany, less than fifty miles from the East German border. In case of war with the Soviet Union, this was the spot where Soviet troops might flood through on their way into central Europe.

In 1959, there was a real threat of war between the United States and its allies and the Soviet Union. Soviet Premier Nikita Khrushchev had threatened to block Allied access to West Berlin. West Berlin was located inside the borders of Soviet-controlled East Germany. Two years later, in 1961, the Berlin Wall was built. The wall stopped East Germans from fleeing to West Berlin. In that same year, the United States and the Soviet Union came close to nuclear war during the Cuban Missile Crisis. The soldiers at Fulda Gap had every reason to believe they might be at the front lines of World War III.

Powell was platoon leader of Company B (Bravo Company), 2nd Armored Rifle Battalion, 48th Infantry. Forty soldiers were under Powell's command.

Through the bitterly cold winters of 1958–59 and 1959–60, Powell sat in his M59 armored personnel carrier with eleven other soldiers guarding the border. They kept watch for signs of Soviet troop movements.

In this first assignment, Powell was called a fine platoon leader by his superiors. In December 1959, Powell was promoted to first lieutenant. In November

1960, his tour of duty in Germany ended. He was sent back to the United States.

First Lieutenant Powell would spend the next two years at Fort Devens, Massachusetts, with the Fifth Infantry Division. The Fifth was a mechanized infantry unit, a unit in which infantry troops move from place to place in the battle area in their own vehicles. While stationed there, Powell's personal life changed dramatically.

Alma Johnson, a young woman from Birmingham, Alabama, was attending graduate school in Boston, Massachusetts. She worked as an audiologist, a person trained in testing people for hearing problems, for the Boston Guild for the Hard of Hearing. Johnson traveled around Boston in a mobile van giving hearing tests to children and adults. When problems were found, the Boston Guild arranged for further tests and medical treatment or hearing aids.

Johnson's college roommate arranged a blind date for her. She did not like the idea of blind dates, but she went along. She especially did not like the idea of blind dates with soldiers.[16] Still, Johnson's roommate convinced her to give it a try. It was in this way that Alma Johnson met Colin Powell in November 1961.

Johnson's first impression was that Powell "looked like he was about twelve years old. He was cold, so his cheeks were rosy, and he had a close haircut, and I thought, all right, who is this baby?"[17] Colin Powell's first impressions were quite different. He recalled being attracted to "a pair of luminous eyes" that were an unusual shade of green.[18] He noticed that this young lady moved gracefully and spoke in a gracious manner with a soft southern accent. For him, the blind date was working out very well.

The couple started to date regularly, often meeting at the Officers Club on base. Alma Johnson liked it there. She appreciated the sense of "community and belonging" and her opinion of Powell quickly improved. "I know [Colin] was a very nice person, probably the nicest person I had ever met," she recalled.[19]

On New Years Day 1962, the young couple enjoyed the holiday with Powell's family. There was dancing, music, much good food, and celebration. Just as she had grown to like Powell, Johnson also liked his family now. It was a warm, loving group of people, and she easily fit in. It proved a joyful time for the young couple, but trouble in a country thousands of miles away was destined before long to upset their happiness.

Colin Powell was promoted to captain in June 1962. In July, he received orders to go to Vietnam. This was not an outpost in the Cold War like Fulda Gap had been. This was a real shooting war. It was also the most brutal kind of war—a civil war.

Powell called parents and friends to tell them about

his new assignment. Though he had some anxiety, he was generally excited to be going to his first war.[20] When he called Alma Johnson with the news, she was interested in just one thing—how would the upcoming separation affect their relationship? At the time Powell knew he cared deeply for Johnson, but he had not thought through the depths of his feelings.[21] He promised Johnson he would write to her faithfully from Vietnam and he hoped she would write back. Johnson surprised him with a blunt answer. "I'm not going to write to you," she said. If they were only to be pen pals, she said, "we might as well end it now."[22]

Powell was forced to come to terms with his own feelings. The couple was facing a twelve-month separation. Johnson was twenty-five and ready for a permanent relationship. Captain Powell had a big decision to make and riding on his next move was his future with the woman he loved.

4

A WEDDING AND VIETNAM

olin Powell lay on his bunk thinking about Alma Johnson. He realized she was all he ever wanted in a wife, and he loved her.[1] He raced to Boston, though without an engagement ring. They would need their money for getting started. Rings would come later. "I said, well, let's get married," Powell recalls, "She said, 'are you asking me?' and I said 'yeah.'"[2]

A big wedding was planned for Captain Colin Powell and Alma Johnson in her hometown of Birmingham, Alabama. Powell's parents were not too eager to enter the South with its racial turmoil.

In the end, the whole Powell family attended the wedding.

It was a hectic time for the newlyweds. Powell remembers, "We got married on a Saturday, spent the night in Birmingham, flew back to Boston on a Sunday, and I was at work Monday."[3] The wedding took place August 25, 1962, eight months after the young couple had met on that blind date.

The Powells were to have just four months together before he left for Vietnam. In October, they moved to Fort Bragg, North Carolina. Powell took six weeks of training in the Army's Special Warfare Center. In December 1962, Alma Powell, now expecting their first child, returned to her parent's home in Birmingham. Powell headed for Vietnam. In a very real sense, both of them would spend the next year in a battleground: Birmingham was in the midst of violent disturbances over civil rights, and a vicious war raged in Vietnam.

Vietnam had been called Indo-China for decades under French rule. In 1954, Communist forces under Ho Chi Minh defeated the French. An international conference held in Geneva, Switzerland, divided Vietnam at the 17th parallel into Communist North Vietnam and non-Communist South Vietnam. By 1958, however, Communist guerrillas in the South, called Viet Cong, were trying to overthrow the South Vietnamese government. American military advisors

Colin Powell and Alma Johnson Powell were married on August 25, 1962, just eight months after they met on a blind date.

Colin and Alma Powell, along with their parents, posed for this photo on the couple's wedding day.

were in South Vietnam to help defend against the Communists. The Americans gave military advice to the South Vietnamese Army, known as the Army of the Republic of Vietnam (ARVN). This would be Captain Powell's mission.

From Saigon, the South Vietnamese capital, Powell traveled north to Da Nang, then to Hue where the First Infantry Division of ARVN had headquarters. Powell would help build leadership and unity in the ARVN. He worked in the rugged, remote mountainous region of A Shau Valley along Rao Loa River, near Vietnam's border with Laos. As Powell prepared to begin his job in this faraway place, his mind and heart were troubled by the violence at home.

Alma Powell and her family were hearing shots fired in anger in Alabama. Powell says of that time:

> My family was living in Birmingham in 1963 when Bull Connor (Birmingham's police chief) and his damn dogs were running up and down the street. I was in Vietnam while my father-in-law was guarding the house with a shotgun . . . so I completely identified with the [civil rights] struggle.[4]

For decades, African Americans had fought against laws that forced them into second-class citizenship. The road to equal rights was long and hard. In the 1950s, the civil rights movement gained new life through people like Martin Luther King, Jr. He led peaceful protest marches against segregation laws that enforced a separation of black and white Americans.

Birmingham was a stronghold of segregation. Their police used tough methods against protestors.

In the spring of 1963, soon after Alma Powell joined her parents in Birmingham, King began leading protest marches in Birmingham. He marched for desegregated public accommodations and equal jobs for all races. The nonviolent marches were met by fire hoses and police dogs. Bombs shattered the home of King's brother, A. D. King. Two more bombs exploded at the headquarters of the civil rights movement in a motel. "To say that Birmingham was a powder keg in 1963 is an understatement," Alma Powell recalled.[5] Between 1957 and 1963, there were eighteen unsolved bombings in African-American neighborhoods in Birmingham. The city was given the grim nickname "Bombingham." Said Alma Powell, "It was ugly. The first bombings took place when I was a child."[6]

In September 1963, an especially tragic bombing took place. The bomb exploded in the bathroom of the Sixteenth Street Baptist Church, a center of the civil rights struggle. Four little girls died in the horrifying attack.

The Johnson home where Alma lived was outside central Birmingham, but it was not outside the danger zone. One day, shortly after the birth of her son Michael, Alma Powell was hanging laundry on the clothesline when gunfire exploded nearby. Her father told her to place the baby in an underground recess below the floor while he stood watch at the window with a shotgun.

Years later, Alma Powell explained how she kept her calm in trying times. "I'm a prayerful person. My prayer is not to make everything come out all right, but, 'Thy will be done, and give us the strength and courage to do whatever it is we are called on to do.'"[7]

Thousands of miles away, Captain Powell did not know he was a father until weeks after the baby's birth. When Powell left for Vietnam, he worked out a plan with his wife to let him know when the baby came. Alma Powell would immediately write a letter with all the details. On the outside of the envelope, she would write the words "baby letter." Powell was usually far away in the most remote outposts on duty. He told the base camp that they should call him on the radio the minute the "baby letter" came. Powell asked that the contents of the letter be read to him. The "baby letter" came, but unfortunately, it was tossed into a large pile of unopened mail where it lay for days.

Powell soon received another letter, this one from his mother. She referred to the birth of the baby but gave no details. She assumed Alma Powell's letter had already arrived. A frustrated Powell radioed the base camp. He wanted all the mail searched for the "baby letter." The letter was finally found and read to him. The young father at last learned that Michael Kevin Powell had been born on March 23, 1963, about three weeks before Powell got word. It would be over six months before Powell would see his newborn son.

While in Vietnam, Captain Powell met the Montagnards, nomadic people who usually lived in the mountains. United States Special Forces organized the Montagnards into a civilian defense group. Their job was to keep North Vietnamese civilians from entering South Vietnam by way of Laos. Powell was surprised to find these mountain people living near base camps like the one at A Shau. The reason was that ARVN troops, wanting to deprive any enemy troops of food, routinely destroyed the fields of corn, onions and manioc that the Montagnards lived on. They had no choice but to rely on the dole.[8]

For weeks, Powell went without contact with another American. A Marine helicopter brought food and mail to the remote outposts. The helicopter usually arrived when Powell was deep in the tropical forest. He searched for signs of the enemy under one-hundred-foot-high trees that formed such a thick canopy overhead that he could go for an entire day without seeing the sun.

Powell's patrols lasted days, even weeks. Over his green fatigues, Powell wore suspenders connected to a web belt. Here he carried ammunition, grenades, and canteens. He carried an M-2 carbine over his shoulder.

Powell walked through muddy quagmires and climbed up steep hills. It was hot and muggy, much

Captain Colin Powell (left) and other soldiers resting during Powell's first tour in Vietnam, in 1963.

like it had been back in Georgia during basic training. Even in the shade, uniforms were soggy with sweat. Powell described moving through clouds of insects. The leeches managed to get through clothing and suck blood from the bodies of the soldiers. Powell could not wear short sleeves in spite of the miserable heat. The razor-sharp elephant grass quickly slashed exposed skin. Still, there were dangers far worse than these in Powell's sector of the war.

The Viet Cong fought a war of ambush. It was a much different kind of war than recent United States military experience in Korea and World War II. No armies clashed on large battlefields. The enemy hid in the thick forest waiting for a chance to strike. Nearly every morning before sunup, the enemy shot at Powell. "They could find us more easily than we could find them," Powell said.[9] The rifle-toting snipers were deadly, as were the mines. Cleverly hidden mines could blow off a limb or blind or kill a soldier. There were also the booby traps that could severely injure anyone who stepped on them in the tall grasses.

In July 1963, as Powell patrolled along a creek bed, he fell victim to a Viet Cong booby trap. A pointy bamboo stick—called a punji stick—its sharp end poisoned with buffalo dung to promote infection, pierced Powell's left instep and came out the top of his foot. The punji stick had been in a small hole about a foot deep.

Powell was a couple hours walk from camp, and he

limped along with the help of a branch made into a crutch, finally reaching the United States Special Forces camp. By this time, his foot was badly swollen and had turned purple as poison from the dung spread. Powell was in great pain as a Medivac helicopter (a military helicopter that evacuated wounded personnel to a hospital) took him to Hue. He recovered quickly from the wound and was soon back on patrol near the Laotian border.

Powell was an excellent officer in his job as advisor. By nature diplomatic and friendly, he was also sensitive to local cultures. He made friends easily with the people with whom he worked. In August, Powell was reassigned to First ARVN Division headquarters as assistant advisor on the operations staff. Powell improved the performance of the division.

Powell was in Vietnam when the South Vietnamese president, Ngo Dinh Diem, was overthrown by a military takeover and then murdered. The war in Vietnam was about to take a turn for the worse.

At the end of 1963, there were about fifteen thousand American troops in Vietnam. Over the next ten years, over 8.5 million Americans would serve in that war. But Captain Powell's tour of duty was over; he was going home. Still, as a soldier, Powell knew he would probably be coming back here. If he did, it would be to a bigger, even more dangerous war. At the time Powell left Vietnam in 1963, he predicted it would take five hundred thousand United States troops to succeed in this mission.[10]

In November 1963, the same month that President John F. Kennedy was assassinated, Powell was reunited with his wife. He met his baby son, Michael, for the first time.

Powell was sent to Fort Benning, Georgia, to attend the Infantry Officers Advanced Course. But the course would not begin for another eight months, so in the meantime Powell was given Advanced Airborne Ranger Training. His big problem was finding decent off-base housing for his wife and son. There was plenty of housing available in the Columbus area for white officers and their families. Powell was limited to the African-American neighborhoods, and he could find nothing as good as the Johnson house in Birmingham where Alma Powell had been living with Michael. So Alma Powell chose to return home with Michael to Birmingham, and Powell stayed at bachelor quarters at the fort. "I was going back and forth to Birmingham every weekend," Powell recalled.[11]

In 1964, the Powells finally found a home—a little brick house in Phenix City, Alabama. It was about ten miles from Fort Benning. Powell was wary at first because Phenix City had a reputation of being a rough town where the National Guard had been called to clean up the crime. Powell saw a bunch of shacks on a back road with a nice brick house in their midst. It had a yard for the baby, and it rented for just $85 a month.[12]

Powell spent February cleaning up the house and making it ready for his family. On his way back to base, he stopped at a small hamburger stand. The waitress looked him over and wondered hopefully if he might be a Puerto Rican. When Powell told her he was an African American, she told him regretfully that he would have to receive his hamburger through the back window. Powell decided he was not that hungry and left the place in a hurry.[13] In fact, Powell could not get a hamburger in half the restaurants off base. On long drives, he could not get a room in most motels either.[14] Segregation was alive and well even for a young American soldier who had just returned from fighting for his country in Vietnam.

The small brick house in Phenix City proved a joyous place. It was the first home the Powells had ever shared as a family. "You can imagine the emotion we brought to it," Powell recalls. "The feelings, the sense of pride, the joy of being together as a family."[15] The house on 28th Avenue in Phenix City has since become famous. In 1993, 28th Avenue was renamed General Colin L. Powell Parkway.

Powell's new job was at the United States Army Infantry Board. He was a test officer with the task of deciding the effectiveness of new equipment. He tested rifles, field packs, and helmets for about seven months, until June 1964. A former colleague remembers him as "very impressive as a soldier. It was in his manner, his demeanor. There was no foolishness, but he was very friendly. He was an intense, hard worker. People liked him."[16]

Powell then trained to be a company commander at Fort Benning, Georgia. The Powell's second child, Linda, was born on April 16, 1965. In February 1966, Powell was called back to infantry school, this time as an instructor. Duty as an instructor was a high honor. Many officers wanted this duty because it looked impressive on a military resume. Instructors were the officers who taught the men who would be leading troops into battle, and the Army chose only the best for the task.

In May 1966, twenty-nine-year-old Powell was promoted to major and was chosen to attend the Army's Command and General Staff College (CGSC). He took a year-long course for experienced majors at Fort Leavenworth, Kansas. Out of a class of 1,244 officers, most older than he, Powell ranked second.

In 1967, the worsening war in Vietnam struck painfully close to home for Colin Powell. His good friend, Major Tony Mavroudis, was killed in action. Years later Powell would visit the Vietnam Veterans Memorial in Washington, D.C., with his Russian counterpart, General Mikhail Moiseyev. Together they searched for and found Mavroudis' name. "And we found his name in the book; we moved to Panel 28 East, and we found his name on the Wall. It was an emotional moment," Powell recalls.[17]

Soon after receiving word that Mavroudis had been

killed, Powell himself got orders to do his second tour of duty in Vietnam. In June 1968, Major Powell was sent to the 3rd Battalion, 1st Infantry Regiment, 11th Infantry Brigade of the 23rd Infantry Division known as the American Division. He was battalion executive officer. His unit was deployed south of Chu Lai in Quang Ngai Province. Powell served in this job for only four months.

General Charles Gettys happened to see an article in *Army Times*. It told about an officer who graduated second at CGSC school, and Gettys was amazed. "I've got the number-two Leavenworth graduate in my division," he cried, "and he's stuck in the boonies. I want him on my staff!"[18]

As battalion executive officer, Powell's job was to make sure the battalion had all the support it needed. His duties included ordering up ammunition, making sure there was enough fuel for the helicopters, and getting mail to the troops. Gettys wanted Powell as one of his own major staff officers. A division commander has five major staff officers, one each for personnel, intelligence, operations and planning, logistics, and civil affairs. Operations and planning is considered the most desirable. Powell became the only major filling that role in Vietnam.

In a near-fatal helicopter crash, it was Major Powell who saved the wounded General Gettys, pulling him from the shattered craft.

Back home in Birmingham, where Alma Powell was waiting out her husband's second tour of duty in Vietnam, she found a letter hanging from her front door. It told her that she had an important telegram. She read the telegram's message—"Your husband has been injured in a helicopter crash."[19] She was given the name of the hospital where he was taken. However, they gave her the wrong hospital, increasing her anxiety. On the subject of war for the loved ones who wait, Alma Powell said:

> We know better than anybody what war brings. It brings deep scars. You absorb a lot of hurt in the process. Things happen to people that you really care about. People die, and as a wife, you always sit at home and wonder if it's your turn.[20]

In fact, during her own long career as an Army wife, Alma Powell did little sitting at home. Always active in volunteer work at whatever base the Powells were stationed, she was one of the hard-working, dedicated women who helped other families as they were forced to cope with constant moving and stresses on family life. Her untiring service in this regard was recognized in 1993 when she received the Army's Decoration for Distinguished Civilian Service.

The war in Vietnam raged on, but in February 1969, Powell was finished with his second tour of duty. He was well, and he was coming home. His life was about to turn in another dramatic direction.

In February, Major Powell was chosen to attend George Washington University in Washington, D.C. He was studying for a master of business administration in data processing. The Army's primary reason for sending Powell into the M.B.A. program was so he might acquire computer skills. Once graduated, he expected he would spend his time at the Pentagon installing computer systems.

During his classes at George Washington University, Powell was back in the civilian world. The Powells bought a single-family, five-bedroom house in Dale City, Virginia, a suburb of Washington. The house cost $31,520, and Powell paid $20 down and $259 a month. At the time he was earning $900 a month, and the mortgage payment proved hard to meet. Major Powell glanced at the *Army Times* and looked at the promotion list for lieutenant colonel. He needed the money.

At Dale City, the Powells were enjoying their first taste of ordinary family life. Events would take place during this time that would make Major Powell more than a military officer of promise. The Powell's third child, Annemarie, was born.

Washington, D.C.—political Washington, D.C.— would soon become a part of his life. It would lead to political power and great opportunities and perhaps a future the thirty-two-year-old soldier never dreamed of.

5

ASSIGNMENT
WASHINGTON AND
BUFFALO SOLDIERS

n Dale City, the Powells joined the local
Episcopalian church, Saint Margaret's, and
became active in parish life. Powell did not
have the opportunity to do this earlier. Soon he was
just another volunteer helping paint the home of the
rector (the clergyman in charge of the parish) on
Saturday mornings. The family took to suburban life
with enthusiasm.

The following summer, Powell was promoted to
lieutenant colonel. In spring 1972, Powell earned his
master's degree with excellent grades. This was
especially sweet since he earned *B*s in some classes he

had flunked at CCNY. Powell was appointed to the Army assistant vice chief of staff's office. He worked very closely with the Army's number three man, General William E. Dupuy. Many talented people worked at the office. The thirty-five-year-old Powell gained a lot from the experience. "It was a hell of a stable," Powell recalled, adding that Dupuy "really fired me up."[1]

Powell wrote some of Dupuy's speeches, and in early 1972, Powell was asked by the Army to apply for a White House fellowship. Fellowships were open to professionals in many fields. Recipients did not work at the White House, but they did get jobs in the executive branch of government at senior levels. It was an outstanding opportunity for someone who would eventually serve in high-level, decision-making jobs.

Powell was given one weekend to answer eight pages of questions. Many of them required two-page answers. Powell was also asked to write a specific policy proposal, keeping it under five hundred words.

One thousand applications were received. Powell made it through the first selection process. He was among the 130 people invited to personal interviews. After the interviews, Powell was among thirty-three national finalists. For three-and-one-half days, Powell and the others were interviewed at a conference center in Virginia. At the end of the weekend, the winners were announced. Powell was one of two African

Americans chosen among the seventeen new White House fellows.

Powell was sent to the White House Office of Management and Budget (OMB) for his year of service. This office creates the annual federal budget. Heading OMB at the time was Caspar Weinberger. Weinberger was destined to play an important role in Powell's life. He admired the bright young lieutenant colonel and became a mentor for Powell. Weinberger and Powell continued to work together over the next decades. In 1990, Weinberger commented on one of the qualities that drew him to Powell. "He is a born leader with whom and for whom people in all walks of life like to work."[2] The deputy at OMB was Frank Carlucci, who would also become a Powell supporter.

At OMB, Powell learned how the federal budget was put together. He learned how numbers were reconciled and conflicts settled. He became an expert in public relations and handling the media. This was a skill he would often use in the future. By the end of the year, Powell had his first taste of Washington, D.C., political life.

In 1973, it was time to return to the Army for a battalion command. Powell took command of the 1st Battalion, 32nd Infantry, 2nd Infantry Division, Eighth Army. The battalion was known as the Queen's Own Buccaneers, shortened to "the Bucs." The battalion had originally been formed in Hawaii when

Queen Liliuokalani ruled in the 1890s. Powell's command would be in Korea where United States troops had been stationed ever since the Korean War (1950–53). It turned out to be a very challenging assignment for Powell.

Lietuenant Colonel Powell found the morale of the Army troops in Korea at rock bottom. Drug abuse and racial hostility between black and white troops raged. Because American soldiers in Korea had no war to fight, the big enemy was boredom. They had nothing to do but go into town where drugs and fights waited.

Powell's second night in camp gave him a bitter taste of the prevailing conditions. Powell was about to go to bed in his Quonset hut when he was urgently called to the provost marshal's office. He came upon a wild scene in which a half-dozen military police (MPs) were trying to subdue a wild private. Powell was told that the private was part of a gang with plans to murder the provost marshal.

Powell was in command of a battalion at Camp Casey, directly north of Seoul and just south of the demilitarized zone (DMZ), a no-man's-land between North and South Korea. Division commander Major General Hank "Gunfighter" Emerson hoped Powell could bring the men in line. The battalion at the time was almost under the control of a military version of a street gang. Emerson believed that if anybody could restore order, it would be an African-American commander.[3]

Lieutenant Colonel Colin Powell served in Korea in 1973. Upon arrival, he found the morale of the troops to be at rock bottom.

Powell immediately studied the men. He formed a close relationship with young company commanders and inspired their confidence. Commented General Emerson, "he [Powell] was charismatic. He really raised the morale, especially the espirit of that unit. It came from very low to very high."[4]

Powell later recalled his plan of action: "I threw the bums out of the Army, and put the drug users in jail. The rest we ran four miles every morning, and by night they were too tired to get into trouble."[5]

Emerson wrote Powell up as one of the two top battalion commanders he had. "He just showed me. I put on his report, this guy should be a brigadier general as quick as the law allows."[6]

In the Korean assignment, Powell was seen as a rough-and-tumble, combat-hardened, no-nonsense kind of guy as well as a nice person.[7] He had taken a unit in the worst possible shape and whipped it into a fine fighting force. He proved himself a first-rate field commander with a fine grasp of how to inspire good people to do their best. He also had the courage to weed out the bad apples. Confronted by an arrogant troublemaker who believed he, not Powell, was in charge, Powell quietly told the man he would be on a plane back to Travis Air Force Base in California that very day, and his discharge papers would be awaiting him.

In the fall of 1974, Powell turned his command in

Korea over to a successor and headed back to the
United States. While he was still in Korea, five
generals held a meeting in Washington to select Army
officers to attend the service war colleges. Attending a
service college is the fourth and final step for an
officer hoping to become a general. The best of these
colleges was National War College—a part of National
Defense University at Fort McNair in Washington,
D.C. Powell was sent there to learn the philosophy and
strategy of war.

Powell was back in the United States in November
1974, and war college would not begin until August
1975. During those nine months, he worked with
career Pentagon officials to prepare a report to
Congress detailing the needs of the four military
services.

When Powell did enter the war college, he was
attending during the time of intense questioning over
the policy of the Vietnam War, so he was in the mood
to learn how wars should not be fought.

Powell studied the eighteenth-century Prussian
military strategist and writer General Carl Von
Clausewitz. In his masterpiece, *On War*, Clausewitz
wrote, "War is nothing but the continuation of policy
by other means."[8] Powell became an adherent of
Clausewitz's theory that waging war effectively needs
three elements: The military must be thoroughly
professional; the policy goals for the war must be

understood by the population; and these goals must be supported by the population. For Powell, these conditions made good sense. He had taken part in a war—the Vietnam War—in which the policy goals were vague and not understood by the people. The only thing the war had going for it was the professionalism and heroic dedication of the military. Powell had witnessed firsthand the bitter results. He would never forget the lessons learned first on the battlefield and then in the classroom at National War College.

Two months before completing his course at National War College, Powell was promoted to colonel. After he graduated, he was sent to Fort Campbell, Kentucky, home of the 101st Airborne Division's 2nd Brigade. His boss's boss was Powell's old friend from Korea, Lieutenant General Hank Emerson. Powell's immediate commander was Major General Jack Wickham. Powell quickly made an excellent impression on Wickham, who said, "Colin was the best brigade commander we had. He was best in his tactical knowledge, in his feel for soldiers, and his ability to communicate."[9]

The Powells returned to Washington in 1979. The new assignment required Powell to be a kind of filter at the Defense Department. He made sure unimportant details did not bog down the desks of high-level people. Powell was soon promoted to brigadier general. In his family life, there were changes too.

Michael Powell, now sixteen, noticed a change in the parental chain of command. "In our house," he recalled, "when you were young, your mother was your primary parent. But at some point the serious life advice started coming from [my dad]."[10] Powell wrote long, heartfelt letters to his son. The twelve-to-fifteen page letters were filled with fatherly advice. It was easier for Powell to give advice to his teenage son in a letter rather than face-to-face. Michael Powell said the family's guiding principles were teaching what was right and what was responsible.[11]

In June 1981, Powell was on the move again. He reported to Fort Carson, Colorado, as assistant commander of the 4th Mechanized Infantry Division. In 1982, Powell was sent to Fort Leavenworth, Kansas. When Powell's former boss, General Wickham, became vice chief of staff in the Army, he asked Powell to help set up Project 14—a think group to help make necessary changes in the Army. Powell took on this task and another quite different project.

Powell's service at Fort Leavenworth led to an unexpected development—the creation of an important and long overdue monument to some of America's finest cavalrymen. One day in 1982, while Powell was jogging at Fort Leavenworth, he wondered if there was a historical monument there honoring the

Colin Powell spent part of 1981 serving at Fort Carson, Colorado. There, he was assistant commander of the 4th Mechanized Infantry Division.

9th and 10th United States cavalries. These were two units of African-American soldiers on horseback formed at Leavenworth and Greenville, Louisiana, in the 1860s. They were dubbed "buffalo soldiers" by the Native Americans they fought in the West. The nickname came from the Native Americans noting the courage of these soldiers matched the spirit of the buffalo, and the soldiers had tight, curly, dark hair like the buffalo. The African-American cavalrymen served until the early 1900s.

Fort Leavenworth was the center of the great western region where the buffalo soldiers served. Since they had carved out such a reputation in blood and courage, Powell thought surely there would be something fitting here in their memory. But when he looked around he found only some gravel back streets named for the 9th and 10th cavalries.

As a student at Command and General Staff College, Powell had formed a friendship with an elderly African-American barber who was a proud veteran of the buffalo soldiers. He learned a lot from him and from reading. The buffalo soldiers were young men recruited after the Civil War (1861-1865) who served in the West primarily during the Indian Wars. As the American frontier constantly moved west into land occupied for centuries by the Native Americans, war broke out. The pioneers in their covered wagons wanted to occupy the land the Native

Americans were using for living and hunting. As the pioneers advanced, the Native Americans fought to defend their land, and many died on both sides. The United States Cavalry, including the buffalo soldiers, were sent in to defend and protect the white settlers.

The buffalo soldiers took part in battles against the Utes, Cheyenne, Sioux, and Apache tribes. Twenty buffalo soldiers received the Congressional Medal of Honor for heroism.

The 9th Cavalry earned the reputation of always being there in the nick of time. In December 1890, in the Black Hills of South Dakota, four companies of the 9th were on a scouting expedition. It was so bitterly cold that their clothing froze to their bodies. They galloped through a heavy gale, ploughing through deep snow to save a settlement from five thousand threatening Oglala Sioux. They rode ninety miles in twenty hours. Then, though worn out, they rode again to relieve the trapped 7th Cavalry, which was battling a Sioux war party. In thirty-four hours, the 9th Cavalry had ridden 108 miles, spent twenty-two hours in the saddle, and fought two battles. They had built one of the most impressive feats of endurance in United States Cavalry history.[12]

The 10th Cavalry took pride in the name "buffalo soldiers" and wore on their uniforms an emblem showing crossed swords, a Native American war bonnet, and a buffalo.[13] Fighting under Captain Louis

Carpenter in 1868, they were called to help drive back a war party of Cheyenne and Sioux at Delaware Creek on the Republican River in Nebraska. The troopers rode one hundred miles to the rescue. They found Major George Forsyth gravely wounded and his men out of food. The 10th Cavalry troopers drove off the warriors and saved Forsyth and his scouts.[14]

Powell was aware of this proud history. He felt in debt to those who came before him. In 1992, he said, "The black soldiers who went before me, but did not have the opportunities I had, are heroes in my eyes."[15]

If there was no suitable monument to these brave men, Powell decided he would correct the oversight. He began to lead a drive to erect a monument at Fort Leavenworth. He talked about the project to friends in Washington, D.C. He urged their financial support.

Finally, an African-American sculptor, Eddie Dixon, was chosen to create the monument. On July 28, 1990, ground was broken for the monument, and General Powell stood on the Kansas hillside to share in the ceremony. Two years later, July 25, 1992, the magnificent monument was dedicated. Powell attended to watch proudly the unveiling of a bronze heroic mounted buffalo soldier with a pond behind him and a reflecting pool and waterfall in front.

At long last, the brave men of the 9th and 10th cavalries had a fitting tribute to the part they played in American history.

Colin Powell led the drive to create a monument to the Buffalo
Soldiers at Fort Leavenworth, Kansas.

The Buffalo Soldier Monument was dedicated on July 25, 1992. Shown here, from left to right, are: Lieutenant General Wilson A. Shoffner, General Colin L. Powell, Retired Colonel Franklin J. Henderson, Governor Joan Finney of Kansas, and Commander Carlton G. Philpot.

Powell displayed on his office wall a painting of the buffalo soldiers as well as a portrait of another African-American soldier, Lieutenant Henry Flipper. Flipper was the first African-American graduate at West Point. He was discharged from the Army on what most believe were false charges after he had served with distinction on the frontier.

In the summer of 1983, another call from Washington came. This time Powell would be moving into a very important high-level, decision-making job.

6

"MR. GORBACHEV, OPEN THIS GATE ... TEAR DOWN THIS WALL"

n July 1983, Brigadier General Colin Powell reported to the Pentagon in Washington, D.C. He was to serve as military assistant to his old friend, now secretary of defense, Caspar Weinberger. Powell was promoted to major general as he went to work in the new administration of President Ronald Reagan.

Powell served Weinberger with total devotion, checking all incoming information so only the most important issues reached Weinberger. One of Powell's greatest skills was conducting effective meetings.

Powell could always cut through trivial material and get to the heart of the matter.

Among the major issues facing the Defense Department at the time was how to build up America's arsenal of weapons by including modern technological advances. They also had to raise military morale. Morale was low because of the long war in Vietnam that did not result in victory. It was also low because Iran held American hostages for a long time, and all efforts to free them failed. They were finally released at the time President Reagan took office. America's military spirit needed a boost. The Defense Department was also dealing with problems in the Middle East and Central America. Containment of the spread of communism in Central America was high on President Reagan's list of priorities.

In Nicaragua, President Anastasio Somoza Debayle had ruled for more than ten years. Because he was not a Communist, he was generally approved of by the United States. But there was much dissatisfaction in Nicaragua with Somoza's rule. In 1979, a rebel guerrilla group called the Sandinistas overthrew Somoza and set up a new government. The Sandinistas began to give aid to rebel guerrillas in neighboring El Salvador. To combat this, the United States began helping anti-Sandinista forces in Nicaragua who were called Contras. The Defense

Department was trying to find ways to keep El Salvador from becoming a Communist nation.

Also at this time, remarkable changes were taking place in the Soviet Union. After more than sixty years as a rigid master of the Communist world empire, a new era dawned. In 1985, Mikhail Gorbachev came to power bringing *glasnost*—the opening and the democratization of the Soviet Union. He also brought *perestroika*—a major reforming of the Soviet government.

Since the end of World War II (1939–1945), two superpowers—the United States and the Soviet Union—had faced each other with more or less hostility and mistrust. Once, in 1962—during the Cuban Missile Crisis—the two nations came to the brink of World War III. Now the Soviet Union was becoming a more democratic Russia, and nations once under Soviet control, like Poland, Czechoslovakia, and East Germany, were independent. The defense plans of the United States had to change too.

Powell helped face this new situation. He wanted to keep America strong and ready for anything. But he did not want to pretend that the old Soviet Union with all its dangers still existed. Michael Pillsbury, assistant under secretary of defense for policy planning, described Powell this way: "He's not a hawk. He's not a dove. He's an owl, in between."[1]

On June 17, 1985, a memo arrived on Powell's

desk that would lead to the incident known as the Iran-Contra affair. The memo was titled "U.S. Policy Toward Iran." It suggested ways of improving United States relations with Iran. Relations had been very poor since 1979 when the leader of Iran, Shah Mohammad Reza Pahlavi, was replaced by Islamic fundamentalists. For many years, the United States had close, friendly relations with the shah, and he was considered a reliable ally of the United States. The Islamic fundamentalists long resented this and blamed the United States for helping the shah remain in power. In November 1979, these fundamentalists vented their bitterness by taking over the United States embassy and holding sixty-two American diplomats hostage.

The memo on Powell's desk proposed that the United States should sell military equipment to Iran. It was suggested that if the United States did not do this, Iran might buy the same materials from the Soviet Union. This would draw Iran into the Communist world.

At this time, American hostages were being held by terrorists in the Middle East. These terrorists had close ties to Iran. Some Americans in the intelligence-gathering area of the government believed we had to deal with Iran to get these hostages out. By selling Iran military equipment, it was hoped the United

States could gain freedom for the hostages as well. This was called the "arms for hostages" deal.

There was still a third element to this deal. Profits gained from selling the military equipment to Iran would be used to fund the Contra struggle against the Nicaraguan government. At this time, the United States Congress was sharply cutting funds to help the Contras, so if money was to be found for this purpose, it would have to be secretly channeled. The Iran-Contra deal was secret, and though it was eventually approved and put into action, President Reagan denied knowledge of it.

Powell sent the memo on to Secretary Weinberger with the recommendation that it be given to Assistant Secretary of Defense Richard Armitage to handle.[2] Weinberger sent the memo back to Powell agreeing that Armitage should handle it. But Weinberger added a handwritten comment on the plans to sell arms to Iran. "This is almost too absurd to comment on," he said.[3]

In spite of Weinberger's total opposition to the "arms for hostages" deal, higher-up officials in the government liked it. The Iran-Contra affair was underway. In mid-January 1986, General Powell was ordered to transfer over forty-five hundred TOW missiles, guided missiles about six feet long that can be fired from military vehicles, from the United States Army stocks to the Central Intelligence Agency (CIA).

Four weeks later, the TOW missiles were flown to Iran. The release of some American hostages followed.

Powell said of Weinberger's role in the whole thing, "The Secretary's record is clear. Weinberger was against it, and did everything he could to oppose it. And I was his companion who tried to help him do that."[4]

Powell said that when he was told to transfer the missiles, "that was my first knowledge that the United States government, at the right level, had approved the transfer of weapons to Iran."[5]

Later there were Congressional investigations of the whole Iran-Contra matter. Senator John McCain of Arizona commented on Powell's role:

> It was a very tough time. They were going through the aid-to-the-contras issues, and a lot of those guys were very badly tarred. Yet he [Powell] was able to conduct himself as he should have. He supported the President and his policies, yet he escaped not only untarred but enhanced. He said it like it is, and he was always scrupulously honest. He never deceived anyone.[6]

Secretary Weinberger was later indicted on Iran-Contra charges for supposedly withholding notes he had from Congress. Powell believed the indictment was a disgrace, and he discussed doing something about it with President Bush.[7] In December 1992, President George Bush pardoned Weinberger.

In June 1986, Powell left Washington again for the traditional Army. He was given command of V Corps in Germany. Powell returned to Germany where as a young officer he had begun his military career. During his first tour of duty, he had commanded forty men. Now he would lead seventy-two thousand troops. Powell was promoted to lieutenant general. (In the Army, the rank of major is higher than lieutenant, but the rank of lieutenant general with the insignia of three silver stars is higher than major general with two silver stars.)

Powell was stationed at Frankfurt, Germany. He was glad to be a soldier again. But the assignment did not last long. Once more the phone rang. Again it was Washington, D.C., calling.

Powell was asked to return to Washington to take over the post of deputy to the new national security advisor, Frank Carlucci. "No way," Powell told Carlucci. "No way."[8] It took a personal call from President Ronald Reagan to get Powell home. "Mr. President," Powell said, "I'm a soldier and if I can help, I'll come."[9]

In January 1987, Powell was back in Washington, D.C., working as a team with Carlucci. They streamlined the National Security Council. Vice-President Bush observed this and said of Powell, "He was crisp and strong."[10]

President Reagan was planning a trip to Germany. Since Soviet leader Mikhail Gorbachev was opening up the Communist world, Powell saw an opportunity to push the opening a little wider. Powell proposed that the president stand at the Brandenburg Gate (next to the Berlin Wall) in West Berlin and deliver these words: "Mr. Gorbachev, open this gate . . . tear down this wall."[11]

Powell believed that since Gorbachev was so anxious to show the world how democratic the Communist world was becoming, Gorbachev would not be able to resist the challenge to smash the wall that divided East Germany from West Berlin. Powell had accurately read how swiftly events were moving. The time was indeed ripe for ending a divided Germany. In November 1989, the Berlin Wall did crumble, allowing the two Germanys eventually to unify.

On June 27, 1987, a personal tragedy struck the Powell family. The Powell's son, Michael, had gone into the Army like his father. He was now a first lieutenant serving in Germany. A Jeep in which he was riding drifted out of control at sixty-miles-per-hour. When the driver tried to regain control, Michael Powell was hurled into the road. The Jeep landed on him. Michael was taken to a German hospital with severe injuries. There seemed little hope of survival. His pelvis was crushed along with part of his lower back. There were also massive internal injuries.

Colin and Alma Powell flew immediately to Germany. In just over a day, Michael Powell needed double the amount of transfused blood as there is in the human body. In critical condition, Michael was flown home to Walter Reed Medical Center in Washington, D.C. Alma Powell remained with him around the clock. General Powell was at his son's bedside part of every day. Both Powells relied heavily on prayer. Powell told his son over and over, "You'll make it. You want to make it, so you *will* make it."[12]

After many surgeries and infections, Michael Powell began to recover. He was in the hospital almost constantly from June 27, 1987, to March 1988. At that time, he was medically retired from the Army with 100 percent disability. Michael, with a somewhat stooped posture because of the back injuries, was able to walk with a cane. During the long hospital stay, he was often visited by his girlfriend, Jane Knott. In October 1988, Michael and Jane were married. They became the parents of the Powell's first grandchild, Jeffrey. In May 1993, Michael Powell graduated from law school at Georgetown University.

In November 1987, Caspar Weinberger resigned as secretary of defense. He was replaced by Frank Carlucci. Left vacant was the post of national security advisor. "With the National Security Council spot open," President Reagan said, "I knew immediately that there could be no better man for the job than Colin Powell."[13]

General Powell became the first African-American

national security advisor (assistant to the president on vital national security issues). Reagan said of Powell, "I have always been appreciative of Colin's candid assessment of situations. Finding someone who will talk straight to you in Washington is a rare and valuable asset."[14]

Powell said of himself in the National Security Council (NSC) job that he was thrust among "all those politicians—me, a soldier!"[15] As national security advisor, Powell coordinated Reagan's five-day Moscow summit in May 1988. Powell did not make radical changes at NSC. He followed in the path set by Carlucci. In his new position, Powell was authoritative, but without a great ego. In group photographs of Reagan and his staff, Powell appeared at the edge of the group, casually dressed, smiling, unflappable, projecting friendliness and charm.[16]

In a 1989 speech, Powell stressed that the future security of the United States and the world depended on a strong international economy. Even the least-developed nations should be included. Powell also urged attention to preserving the world's environment. He was concerned about ozone depletion and deforestation. Powell strongly opposed high tariffs and trade wars among nations. Then he turned to a favorite subject—education. He called education the backbone of a strong economy. Nations needed an educated workforce to compete. This is a theme that recurs in Powell's speeches wherever he goes. It comes out most strongly when he is talking to young people. He literally barks out to students that he is giving them an order. "Stay in school! Stick with it!"[17]

Vice President George Bush was elected president in 1988, and Powell thought he would not be staying on at NSC. Powell knew Bush, and they had a good relationship. But he was not as close to Bush as he had been to Reagan. Powell assumed Bush would want his own person in the NSC spot. Powell was not even sure he wanted to stay on if asked. He was at another crossroads in his career. He could not foresee that in a few months he would again make history.

7

"God Gave Us Life to Use for a Purpose"

n November 9, 1989, President-elect George Bush had a talk with General Colin Powell about his future. Bush implied someone else would be taking over Powell's current job. Then he offered Powell the top spot at the Central Intelligence Agency (CIA). Bush himself had once held this position as "top spy"; Bush enjoyed it, and he thought Powell might, too. Powell did not want it. Nor did Bush's second offer appeal to him—the number two spot at the State Department, which is deputy secretary. Powell told Bush that the military was his career, and he was a soldier first.[1] It looked like the Powells would soon be leaving Washington.

In April 1989, Powell was assigned to Forces Command at Fort McPherson, Georgia. Called FORSCOM, Powell's command included a quarter million active duty troops, another quarter million reservists, and a half million National Guard soldiers in training. Powell was always on the road visiting the various divisions, and he came to know the generals in every command.[2] Powell also received his fourth star, making him a four-star general.

When Powell reached Fort McPherson, he was surprised to find that many of the military he came in contact with were not preparing for a post-Soviet world.[3] After all, the Soviet Union's empire was crumbling rapidly. Communist states fell throughout East Europe. "The bear looks benign," Powell quipped in the spring of 1989.[4] He even thought some of the former Communist states might soon be applying to join the North Atlantic Treaty Organization (NATO— once formed to defend against Communist aggression).[5]

On Sunday, August 6, 1989, while on a plane to Baltimore, Powell saw a newspaper story describing a so-called scramble to select a new Chairman of the Joint Chiefs of Staff. The article listed Powell and General Robert Herres of the Air Force as the leading contenders for the job. The current chairman was Admiral William J. Crowe, Jr. The post rotated among the Army, Navy, and Air Force. Of the eleven men serving prior to 1989, five had been from the United States Army, and three each from the Air Force and Navy. The chairman of the joint chiefs is the primary military advisor to the president.

In spite of the article, Powell did not believe he would be chosen. For one reason, Admiral Crowe was said to favor Herres. Frank Carlucci, however, supported Powell, calling him one of Washington's best problem-solvers. Secretary of Defense Richard Cheney was carefully weighing the pros and cons of each candidate.

On the negative side, Powell was the most junior of the four-star generals who were eligible. Cheney as well as President Bush had concerns that the more senior men might resent the elevation of a man junior to them.[6] Powell had been a four-star general for only six months. Would the other generals feel they had been jumped over? On the positive side were a wealth of recommendations throughout Powell's career pointing to this person as someone of unusually outstanding qualities.

On suggestions that Powell's race played an important role in the selection, retired Colonel Ben Willis scoffed, saying Powell would have made it to the top "if he was purple."[7]

At last, Cheney met with Powell for the purpose of discussing the job. He was not sure if Powell was even interested in the job if offered. Certainly Powell never campaigned for it. Powell was to say later, "I didn't refuse this job, but neither did I go out looking for it."[8]

Powell told Cheney he would be interested in the post but had no great ambition for it. Cheney was impressed with Powell. He went to President Bush and told him he thought Powell should be the next Chairman of the Joint Chiefs. Bush accepted the recommendation and made the appointment.

At fifty-two, Powell was the youngest person ever chosen as chairman. He was also the first African American. Prior to this moment, every important leadership position in foreign policy and national defense was handled exclusively by white men. In the case of Powell, the white power structure had decided to place the safety and future of the United States in the hands of an African American. His judgments would resolve grave decisions, and he would guard vital secrets few would ever know.[9] This was a remarkable breakthrough.

For more than two hundred years, African Americans had served in every American war since the American Revolution. Still, it was not until the 1950s that President Dwight Eisenhower completed the desegregation of the armed forces begun by President Harry Truman. After thousands of African Americans had served and died in these wars, an African-American general would be making vital decisions about them.

During the ceremony installing him as Chairman of the Joint Chiefs, General Powell made reference to a famous painting that shows a military family at prayer. The father is in uniform. Powell said that every time he sees the painting "a silent prayer comes to mind for all who serve this nation in times of danger. Beneath the painting there is an inscription from the prophet Isaiah. The words read 'And the Lord God asked "whom shall I send? Who will go for me?" And the reply came back: "here Am I, send me."'" Powell went on to say that he felt that was the essence of military service. "That's the ultimate statement of selfless service. Send me."[10]

Powell quickly put his personal stamp on the office of chairman. He brought tapes of the varied music he enjoys—Carly Simon, Benny Goodman, Strauss waltzes, Louis Armstrong, the Statler Brothers, Mozart, Paul Simon, and Count Basie.[11]

Powell's mementoes took their place in his office, reflecting his interests and his long career. He had long been collecting and rebuilding Volvo automobiles, often selling them to friends. So a brass model of a 1927 Volvo sat on his desk. A shotgun, given to Powell by Soviet leader Mikhail Gorbachev, shared space with a chunk broken off during the destruction of the Berlin Wall.

The doorknob from one of Morris High School's classrooms, Powell's alma mater, was displayed with a baseball card bearing the likeness of World War II B-17 bomber pilot, Colin P. Kelly, Jr., who won the Distinguished Service Cross after dying in an attack on a Japanese battleship after Pearl Harbor. Kelly was a popular hero of the time, and so Powell remembers being Colin of Kelly Street to his friends in that era.

A framed quotation from President Abraham Lincoln hanging in Powell's office seemed perfect for deflating egos. "I can make a brigadier-general in five minutes, but it is not easy to replace one-hundred-and-ten horses."[12]

Powell liked aphorisms (brief statements containing a truth). He kept them around his office to remind himself to follow his own favorite advice, such as: "Have a vision. It ain't as hard as you think. Don't take the counsel of your fears, or naysayers. Remain calm. Be kind. It will look better in the a.m. Share credit. Get mad, then get over it."[13]

In Powell's office also was the bust of a person he greatly admired—Thomas Jefferson. Powell refers warmly to Jefferson as T.J. He admires him because he helped launch a great nation. He also admires President Abraham Lincoln because he freed the slaves. And Powell's third hero is Martin Luther King, Jr. "Lincoln freed the slaves," Powell said, "but Martin Luther King set the rest of the nation free."[14]

General Powell has a strong personal faith in God. He describes his religious attitude in this way: "I'm a dyed-in-the-wool unreformed Episcopalian of the 1928 Prayer Book."[15] In recent years, the Episcopalian Church revised their prayer book, and Powell often expresses his preference for the old ways.

As a soldier, Powell attended Episcopalian services every Sunday and then went to the base chapel to attend different religious services. He wanted to share the religious experiences of his men, so sometimes he went to a black Baptist service, other times to a Catholic Mass. Powell once wrote that he believed "God's watching over me."[16]

Powell describes his personal credo in this way:

> I believe in the country we live in; I believe in the system we have in this country; I believe in the fundamental goodness of people; I believe in my family. I believe in myself; I believe that God gave us life to use for a purpose.[17]

Powell brought to the job of chairman his steady personality. Alma Powell describes her husband as "the calmest person I know. He's a man of few words."[18] She said she never could tell from his mood if a serious crisis was underway. She would find out rather from the number of phone calls he got. When they came flooding in, she knew something was boiling over in the world.

For entertainment, the new chairman watched old movies. He also enjoyed working on his old Volvos. Alma Powell said he prefers eating a peanut-butter-and-jelly sandwich to dining out.[19] Powell's other favorite foods include cold-cut sandwiches, soups, diet colas, and hamburgers.

When Powell was appointed chairman, he was asked what about the job gave him the greatest satisfaction. He said:

> It's been enormously flattering to me to see the reaction from the Black community. It's been a source of great pride to walk into a store and have a Black young man come up and say, "I just wanted to shake your hand." Or to drive through a parking lot . . . and have somebody chase me down to get a signature.[20]

Powell said he was eager to give hope to others, hoping African Americans will say, "Hey, look at that dude. He came out of the South Bronx. If he got out, why can't I?"[21]

Although General Powell was not installed as chairman until October 3, 1989, during a large ceremony on the green outside the Pentagon, he was already on the job days earlier. A crisis was underway, and Powell was trying to solve it. A coup had occurred in Panama in Central America, and vital American interests were at stake.

8

PANAMA TO
PERSIA

n May 1989, elections in Panama had apparently defeated the candidate chosen by General Manuel Noriega. Noriega was known by the United States military to be a tyrant and a drug dealer. The military thought Noriega made a lot of money helping illegal drugs get into the United States. Washington, D.C., was glad to see Noriega go. They hoped the new government would be more democratic. They also hoped Panama would stop being a source of drugs. But then Noriega quickly nullified the election results. The winning candidates were beaten up and driven into hiding. It was going to be business-as-usual in Panama. Noriega was still in charge.

Just as General Powell was taking office as Chairman of the Joint Chiefs of Staff, Panamanians were staging a coup in the hopes of deposing Noriega. The Panamanian people wanted the leaders they had elected into office to take charge. Some in the United States wanted to pitch right in and help the Panamanian enemies of Noriega. They saw this as a great chance to return democracy to Panama and arrest Noriega on drug charges.

Powell studied the situation. He advised against American involvement at that time because the situation in Panama was too unpredictable. The United States could not be sure that democracy would be restored as a result of the coup. This was to be a hallmark of Powell's policy—to move militarily only with great strength and with a great likelihood of gaining the objectives.[1]

Powell briefed President Bush on the situation. The president took Powell's advice, and the United States did not enter into the Panamanian struggle at that time. There were angry complaints in Washington about that. Some said that the United States had missed a great chance because of a lack of courage. Powell kept his cool. He methodically planned for when the United States *would* be ready to actively play a role in solving the crisis in Panama. But before that happened, there were other problems with which to deal.

In November 1989, President Corazon Aquino's shaky three-and-one-half-year-old Philippine government was in major trouble. A gentle revolution in 1986 had ousted longtime ruler Ferdinand Marcos. Many hoped that Aquino could solve the nation's serious economic problems. But now, three thousand members of the military mounted a coup against Aquino. Rebels took over the military bases and television stations. Rebel planes shot at the presidential palace. Aquino asked for United States assistance, but what form would it take? Some in the Bush administration urged the immediate bombing of the airfields where rebel planes landed and took off.

General Powell urged President Bush to be careful. He warned the president that if American bombs killed Filipinos, no one in that country would forgive the United States.[2] Powell's plan was to take action short of bombing. He asked that United States planes were to fire warning shots at rebel T-28s taxiing to take off and to shoot them down if they did take off. Bush again took Powell's advice. The plan was successful. By early December, the coup was over. Powell keeps a quote by the Athenian historian Thucydides handy, "Of all manifestations of power, restraint impresses men most."[3]

The philosophy of restraint urged by Powell had served the United States in the Philippines well. Powell knew that to use massive force quickly in a crisis was like burning down a house to get rid of termites.

In December 1989, the situation in Panama was once more at crisis stage. Marine Lieutenant Robert Paz was shot and killed in Panama. Powell was immediately informed. It was clear that conditions in Panama were rapidly falling apart. American citizens were under attack. After consulting with Secretary of Defense Cheney and his staff, Powell went to President Bush with a clear plan of action. It was now time to invade Panama and throw out the illegal government. Noriega would be arrested and brought to trial on drug charges. Democracy would be brought to Panama.

Powell frankly told Bush, "We are going to own the country [of Panama] for several weeks."[4] Powell warned that there would be casualties and chaos, but in the end, the objectives would be gained. The United States had sufficient forces in the area and a well-thought-out plan to do the job right.

Bush launched Operation Just Cause, the name given the invasion of Panama, on December 20, 1989. As the reason for the action, Bush cited the grave threat to the safety of thirty-five thousand Americans living in Panama. He also spoke of dangers to the Panama Canal and its vital role in world commerce.

The powerful military force assembled was the largest United States operation since Vietnam.[5] The Air Force, Army, Marines, and Navy were involved. Twelve thousand United States troops were already in Panama. They were quickly joined by about twelve thousand rangers, paratroopers, and other military. The combined troops were organized into five task forces—including the first-ever combat use of the F-117 Stealth fighter.

The invasion began at midnight, and by 2:00 A.M., United States forces had taken the Panamanian defense headquarters. Hostilities lasted for about four days, but the United States troops remained there in a peacekeeping operation for much longer. For the first time in history, the operation of the Panama Canal had been suspended for one day.

Twenty-three Americans were killed, and over three hundred were wounded. The Panamanian toll was far greater, including hundreds of soldiers and civilians killed in the fighting. Noriega was eventually captured. He was brought to trial in the United States, where he was convicted of drug trafficking charges and sent to prison. A more-democratic government was installed in Panama. Operation Just Cause was generally called a big success.

In July 1990, there were rumblings of much more serious trouble in the world. General Powell had expected that sooner or later we would have to intervene in Panama, and we were well prepared. But the growing crisis in the Persian Gulf, between Saudi Arabia and Iraq in the Middle East, was something unexpected. The Iraqis, under President Saddam Hussein, were building troop strength on the border of small, oil-rich Kuwait. Was Iraq preparing to attack Kuwait, an ally of the United States? Or, worse yet, would Iraqi troops race across Kuwait and then invade Saudi Arabia? This would threaten a major source of the world's oil.

On July 24, Powell called General H. Norman Schwarzkopf at MacDill Air Force Base in Tampa, Florida. If the United States were to get involved in the Middle East, it would be in Schwarzkopf's area of command. As commander-in-chief (CINC) or central command (CENTCOM), Schwarzkopf was responsible for the Middle East. Powell and Schwarzkopf had met five years earlier when they were both at Fort Myers, Virginia. When Powell became national security advisor, Schwarzkopf was Army operations deputy.

Both Powell and Schwarzkopf agreed on the world's problems. They believed that since the threat of the Soviet Union had lessened, the United States should prepare for a smaller military. They were both hard-headed and realistic about what it takes to mount a successful military operation.

Powell asked Schwarzkopf if he thought Iraq was about to invade Kuwait. If so, would Iraq make a

General Colin Powell meets with General H. Norman
Schwarzkopf regarding the Allied military coalition during
Operation Desert Shield.

🗆🗆🗆🗆🗆🗆🗆🗆🗆🗆🗆🗆🗆🗆🗆🗆🗆🗆🗆🗆🗆🗆🗆🗆🗆🗆🗆🗆🗆🗆🗆🗆

limited attack within Kuwait's borders, or would they take over Kuwait? Schwarzkopf believed a limited attack was most likely. Powell began to plan strategy for whatever happened.

By July 27, 1990, Powell was still hoping the Iraqi troop buildup was just saber rattling (bluffing) and no invasion was near. Saudi ambassador Prince Bandar and others talked to Powell on July 30. They seemed to agree that Saddam Hussein would not invade Kuwait. But then his Iraqi army was on the move again. It looked like as many as one hundred thousand Iraqis were closing in on the Kuwait border.

On August 1, Powell urged President Bush to issue a warning to Saddam Hussein through diplomatic channels that he faced grave consequences if he invaded Kuwait. Before Bush could do this, at 9:00 P.M. on August 1, news reached the world that Iraqi forces were rolling across Kuwait's border. Iraqi tanks were nearing the capital, Kuwait City.

General Powell received the grim news at his home. At 6:00 A.M., August 2, Powell was at his office in the Pentagon. President Bush hoped the invasion would be reversed by diplomacy, but he was very uncertain about the outcome.[6] Once the Iraqi army swept across Kuwait, what was to stop them from invading Saudi Arabia? Saddam Hussein could gain control of a dangerously high percentage of the world's oil. He could, in effect, hold the world hostage to his demands.

Powell helped brief the United States senators on defense committees about the fast-moving events. Then he met with the joint chiefs. On August 4, Powell and others flew to Camp David to give President Bush his military options.

Schwarzkopf was at the meeting, and he laid out the Iraqi strengths. He said they were a tough army. Powell saw the main problem of the moment to be preventing the invasion of Saudi Arabia. A United States land force had to be quickly placed in Saudi Arabia. Saddam Hussein must know at once that if he sent troops into Saudi Arabia he would be taking on the United States. This operation—dubbed Operation Desert Shield—was agreed upon.

On a hot August afternoon, Powell was watching television when he saw President Bush's helicopter land on the White House lawn. After some questions from reporters, the president declared in an angry voice that he viewed the occupation of Kuwait very seriously. And then he said, "This will not stand. This will not stand—this aggression against Kuwait."[7] Powell realized that in these emotion-charged moments, the president had changed the goals of the United States. The United States was not only determined to prevent the invasion of Saudi Arabia, but another goal had also been added. President Bush planned to liberate Kuwait.[8]

That evening Powell was back at the White House making sure he heard what he thought he heard. Had Bush really changed the goals? Operation Desert Shield was underway, and yes, the United States was going to liberate Kuwait. Speaking from the Oval Office on August 8, 1990, Bush said, "We seek the immediate, unconditional and complete withdrawal of all Iraqi forces from Kuwait."[9] As to why the president made this decision keeping his own counsel, Powell speculated that it was characteristic of Bush to listen to his advisors and then sometimes to reach momentous decisions on his own.[10]

The United Nations swiftly approved economic sanctions against Iraq in retaliation for the invasion of Kuwait. Then on August 25, the United Nations Security Council voted to give the United States and its allies the right to use force to set up a blockade of Iraqi shipping.

As Operation Desert Shield's thousands of American forces took their places beside Saudi Arabian troops in the Arabian Desert, it became clear that Saddam Hussein did not plan to withdraw from Kuwait.

In September 1990, General Powell visited the United States troops in Saudi Arabia. Then he returned home to describe to President Bush the

General Colin Powell greets a Marine during a visit to inspect various units of the 7th Marines deployed during Operation Desert Shield.

containment strategy for driving Iraqi forces from Kuwait. This strategy was to blockade Iraq and keep them from trading with other nations, thereby bringing their economy to a halt. It was hoped that the resulting economic troubles would force Iraq to pull out of Kuwait. President Bush did not think this would work quickly enough. He wanted Iraq out of Kuwait—and soon. By early October, the president was planning military action to force Iraq from Kuwait.

General Schwarzkopf had tens of thousands of troops in the desert for Desert Shield, but he did not have enough for a major war. Schwarzkopf wanted to be sure he would have enough personnel and materials to do the job before an attack was ordered. In October 1990, Powell and Schwarzkopf huddled in Saudi Arabia to work on an offensive plan. Powell pledged to Schwarzkopf that he would get all that he needed in troops and equipment. "If we go to war," Powell told Schwarzkopf, "we will not do it halfway. The United States military will give you whatever you need to do it right."[11]

On Monday, October 30, Bush met with his advisors, including Powell. Powell reported that Desert Shield had worked. Saudi Arabia was secure. Then Powell told the president what forces Schwarzkopf would need to drive the Iraqi army from Kuwait, if that was the president's goal. Schwarzkopf would need double the forces he now had. Although some of the others at the meeting gasped at the huge demand, Bush did not hesitate. "If that's what you need, we'll do it," he said.[12] Powell had kept his promise to Schwarzkopf. Americans would not be sent into war without the means to win.

On November 29, 1990, the United Nations Security Council voted 12–2 to authorize force to drive Iraq from Kuwait. Only Yemen and Cuba opposed, and China abstained. Hussein was given a deadline for the withdrawal—January 15, 1991. On Saturday, January 12, Congress, after three days of sober debate, granted Bush the authority to go to war. The Senate vote was 52–47. The House vote was 250–183.

On January 15, 1991, Powell had a phoncom [secure phone and fax line] conversation with Schwarzkopf to advise him that he and the secretary of defense had signed the order for the attack to begin at 0300 January 17. He told Schwarzkopf that a single copy of the order would be faxed immediately.[13] Operation Desert Shield would become Operation Desert Storm.

In the Persian Gulf, the U.S.S. *Bunker Hill* fired a Tomahawk long-range missile into Iraq. Twenty Tomahawks were programmed to hit Hussein's presidential palace, the main telephone exchange, and Baghdad's electric power-generating stations. There were one thousand air sorties (flights) in the

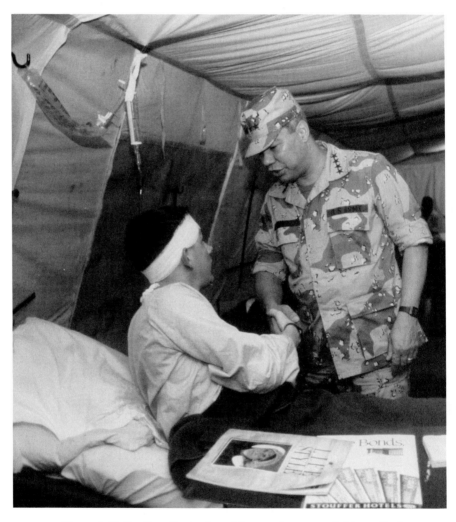

General Colin Powell speaks with a patient at a field medical facility during Operation Desert Shield.

first twenty-four hours. Operation Desert Storm was underway.

General Powell remained alone in his office, sitting in a large maroon chair. His final conversation with Schwarzkopf ended with a simple, "Good luck, Norm."[14] After the war was going for a week, Powell gave a briefing. "Our strategy for dealing with the [Iraqi] army is very simple," he said. "First we're going to cut it off, and then we're going to kill it."[15]

Powell had worked hard on the bombing campaign to keep damage to nonmilitary targets to a minimum. There was restraint shown. There was no desire to destroy Iraq.

The Persian Gulf War lasted forty-two days. The air war phase lasted thirty-eight days, and the ground war phase lasted just over four days. President Bush then declared a cease-fire. The United States and its allies overran Kuwait and the southern part of Iraq. Saddam Hussein's army was destroyed. His elite Republican Guard was routed. American casualties totalled 147 killed in battle and 236 dead of noncombat causes.[16] Tens of thousands of Iraqis died.

Colin Powell was seen as the chief architect of Desert Storm and Norman Schwarzkopf as its chief executor.[17] Americans broke out yellow ribbons and millions of American flags to welcome home the victorious heroes.

In the many parades and celebrations held to

Secretary of Defense Richard Cheney, General Colin Powell, and General Norman Schwarzkopf stand during an award ceremony prior to the Welcome Home parade honoring the coalition forces of Operation Desert Storm.

celebrate the Gulf War victory, thoughts returned to Vietnam. When the troops returned from the Vietnam War, more than a decade earlier, they received no such warm welcome. Often military people were met by anger and resentment, not gratitude. So in the Gulf War parades, groups of Vietnam War veterans were included. It was the nation's way of saying they were sorry about how the Vietnam veterans had been treated. This celebration was for them, too. America had a victory to celebrate, and among the new heroes was General Colin Powell. Fittingly, he was also a Vietnam War veteran.

9

A GREAT PATRIOT

I n 1991, General Powell was reappointed to a second term as Chairman of the Joint Chiefs of Staff. On January 20, 1993, a new president, Bill Clinton, took office. Powell would not be in the inner circle of this new administration. Although Powell had a cordial relationship with Clinton, a major controversy would soon divide the two men. Clinton had pledged during the 1992 campaign to lift the military ban on homosexual personnel. Early in his presidency, he sought to fulfill that promise. General Powell disagreed with changing the long-standing policy.

General Powell frankly told the president that in order to preserve good order and discipline in the military, it would be necessary to maintain a ban on homosexuals. He said that the military life was very much unlike ordinary society. Soldiers lived together twenty-four hours a day, especially in combat situations. "I believe the privacy rights of all Americans in uniform have to be considered," Powell said.[1]

Powell's position was supported by the other service chiefs, who said they had consulted with their field commanders and troops and the majority of them opposed lifting the ban.[2]

The concerns of Powell and the others in the military led Clinton to modify his position. A new policy toward homosexual personnel was established. It was nicknamed "don't ask, don't tell." It meant the military would not ask service personnel about their sexual orientation and personnel would not volunteer the information either. Homosexual personnel who did make their orientation public could not remain in the service. This was quite different from the policy Clinton had advocated during his campaign.

Powell's second term as chairman ran out on September 30, 1993. He believed it was time to move on from the Army to other things. In an emotional farewell, he paid tribute to the profession he loved. "I am where I am today," he said, "because the Army

Sideboys salute in September 1992, as General Colin Powell and Admiral Paul D. Miller come aboard to tour the amphibious assault ship U.S.S. *Wasp.*

takes care of its own. I was allowed to rise based on my performance."[3]

Powell retired from the military after thirty-four years as a career officer. "But I've never in the past thirty-four years found any other line of work, profession, or any other livelihood that appealed to me more than being a soldier," he said.[4]

After little more than a year out of the public eye, Powell was called upon by President Clinton to help in a new crisis. He was asked to join Senator Sam Nunn of Georgia and former President Jimmy Carter on a mission to Haiti.

The democratically-elected Haitian president, Bertrand Aristide, had been driven from office by a military coup led by General Raoul Cedras. Conditions in Haiti had grown desperate. Reports of killings, riots, and hunger spread. Clinton demanded that Cedras step down and allow Aristide to return to the presidency. If Cedras would not step down, President Clinton had decided to intercede. An American invasion force assembled outside Haiti to enforce these demands. If the mission of Powell and the others was successful, the American troops could enter Haiti without bloodshed. Otherwise they would have to shoot their way in.

General Cedras believed it would be shameful for him to flee the country under threat of a United States invasion.[5] His wife, Yanick, said, "We will die before we leave Haiti."[6] Powell met with Cedras and his wife and spoke in dramatic and heartfelt language. Powell told Cedras that when a mission is impossible, it is the duty of a commander to protect the lives of his soldiers. Powell told him a good commander does not sacrifice his soldiers in a hopeless cause. Cedras and his wife listened intently. It was, Senator Nunn said, "a very strong and, I think, decisive argument."[7]

General Powell spoke to Cedras soldier-to-soldier. "We've got youngsters coming in here tomorrow morning," he said, "and I need to know they won't meet resistance."[8] Cedras promised his army would not block the American landing. He gave his word as a soldier. "I knew he meant it," Powell said, "so we were able to go forward."[9]

After the deal with General Cedras was signed, a Clinton aide said, "Jimmy Carter headed the delegation, but everyone knew Colin Powell was the most important person on that plane."[10] Powell had the military background to convince Cedras. He could vividly describe America's overwhelming firepower and convince Cedras that resistance was futile.

While in the military, Powell felt a great sense of responsibility, especially to the young. Addressing a mostly African-American graduating class at Fisk University, he said:

> We must all reach back, we must all reach down. We
> must all work together to pull our people, to pull all

Americans out of the violence, out of the dark, soul draining world of drugs, out of the turmoil in our cities. As we climbed on the backs of others, so must we allow our backs to be used for others to go higher than we have.[11]

As Powell moved into civilian life, he continued to work as a force for good. In the words of former boss, Caspar Weinberger, Powell is "a great patriot in the best and truest sense of the word."[12]

Long a sought-after speaker, Powell traveled around the United States in 1995 giving an eloquent message of sacrifice, hard work, pride, and love of family and country. His words appeared to be well received by inner-city youth as well as midwestern conservatives. His philosophy has been described as a "brilliantly balanced mix of conservative values and a somewhat liberal view of the proper role of government."[13] Powell sees America as a big family just as he viewed the military as a family with each member looking out for the others. A favorite anecdote of his tells of an African-American soldier being interviewed right before American forces went into battle in Desert Storm. The soldier was asked if he was afraid of the fight ahead. "He said, 'I am not afraid. And the reason I'm not afraid is that I'm with my family.'" Then, as Powell tells the story, the African-American soldier looked back over his shoulder at the others in the unit. "They were white and black and yellow and every color of the American mosaic. The soldier said 'that's my family. We take care of one another.'"[14]

Powell stresses that concept of family everywhere he goes. "We've got to start remembering," he said, "that no member of our family should be satisfied if any member of our American family is suffering or in need and we can do something about it."[15]

Since leaving the office as Chairman of the Joint Chiefs, Powell has been enjoying his home in the Washington, D.C., suburb of McLean, Virginia. He calls himself "General Harry Homeowner" and pitches in personally for such chores as repairing water damage to drywall when an upstairs shower ran over. Memos he sends to his office often bear engine grease stains from time spent working on Volvos at home.[16] Best of all, Powell has finally had the chance to enjoy his family at leisure. Son Michael lives nearby with his wife, Jane, and his sons Jeffrey and Bryan. Older daughter Linda, long interested in an acting career, now appears regularly in plays. She graduated from a two-year program at the Circle in the Square theater in Manhattan and made her Broadway debut in Thornton Wilder's retrospective, *Wilder, Wilder, Wilder.* Younger daughter Annemarie graduated from The College of William and Mary and has worked on various news programs, including *Nightline.*

Alma Powell, always a tireless volunteer throughout her husband's military career, sits on the Kennedy

Center board, works with the Red Cross and CARE (Cooperative for American Relief Everywhere), and finds time to make sandwiches at a Washington soup kitchen.

Beginning in earnest in 1995 were serious discussions about Colin Powell running for president of the United States. Old friend Harlan Ullman said he was not sure what the future held for Powell, "but I would tend to be of the school that the future holds something far, far greater."[17]

Political experts, Republicans, Democrats, and independents were talking about Powell as a formidable candidate. Ordinary Americans were becoming more inspired than many had been in a long time. Vietnam veteran Gaylord Stevens was a young boy when his own father had taken him to hear President John F. Kennedy speak. In May 1995, Stevens brought his own son in his Boy Scout uniform to San Antonio, Texas, to hear Powell speak. Stevens said of Powell, "If he becomes President, we would have a dream again."[18] That seemed to be the heart of hopes that Powell would become a presidential candidate—that he offered the chance to raise politics to a higher level.

10

MY AMERICAN
JOURNEY

he first soldier to be seriously considered as
a presidential candidate in forty years (since
General Dwight D. Eisenhower was
president), Powell has never seemed politically
ambitious. "I have no political fire in my belly," he said
once.[1] Another time he said, "I would rather be
president than a presidential candidate when you look
at what is required to win an election."[2]

In an article he wrote for his college magazine in
1988, Powell said:

> I was 21 years old in Fort Benning, Georgia before I
> ever saw what is referred to as a White Anglo-Saxon

Protestant. So it was somewhat of an advantage for me
to enter the Army without realizing I was a "minority."
And if there's one thing I've tried to do over the many
years that followed is to allow the fact of my minority
status to be somebody else's problem, not mine.[3]

This attitude as well as the circumstances of his life
have created in Powell a unique individual. He is an
African American who looms so large that the race
issue seems transcended. In fact, for Powell, being
African American became a plus. In mid-July 1995,
Paul Sniderman, a Stanford University political
science professor, said his national polls on Powell's
race actually "magnifies his political strength."[4]
Sniderman said that when white voters find someone
like Powell who flies in the face of negative racial
stereotypes "their response is to respond even more
positively to him."[5]

What about Powell's appeal in the African-
American community? Historian Russell L. Adams
said there exists "considerable pride in Powell's public
elevation and skepticism about the degree to which he
would be able to assist them (African Americans)."[6]
This skepticism derives from the long association
Powell has had with Republican administrations.

As interest in Powell's presidential candidacy grew
toward the fall of 1995, his long-awaited biography,
My American Journey, was published. In September
1995, Powell made a twenty-three-city, twenty-day
publicity book tour including print media and

television interviews. Record crowds met Powell at every bookstore.

Powell's positions on issues also became more clear as he answered direct questions. He opposed organized prayer in school but had no problem with a moment of silence. Abortion, he said, was a matter between a woman "her doctors, her family, and her conscience and her God."[7] But he remained vague on many other issues like welfare reform, affirmative action, and how to resolve the national debate on entitlements. Political writers again compared him to President Eisenhower, who had said, "Embracing detailed positions would alienate more strength than it would develop."[8] Eisenhower urged candidates to avoid specifics. Powell did indeed appear to be "just like Ike," not only in popularity but in style.

Tantalizing his supporters in September 1995, Powell gave this reply to the question, do you feel confident you could handle the presidency?: "Yes. I think I have the skills to handle the job."[9] Powell promised a definite decision soon. He indicated that if he ran it would be as a Republican.

As the moment of decision neared, Powell soared in the polls. Former President Gerald Ford called Powell "the best public speaker in America."[10] Here was a man with a chance to unite America, heal racial divisions, and revive trust in government. One political writer described Powell as "a black man on a white horse."[11]

For Powell, it was a time of family discussions and agonizing self-examination. Did he really want to be president? Son Michael Powell said, "I have never in my life seen him so torn up about something."[12]

During family discussions, Alma Powell and their daughters generally opposed a presidential campaign while son Michael leaned in favor. When someone in the family would turn to Colin Powell and ask, "What do you want to do?" he would answer, "I don't know."[13]

As Draft Powell committees sprang up, congresspersons and governors expressed an eagerness to endorse him, and fund-raisers began setting up timetables, Powell met in earnest with three people. Alma Powell and two old friends and colleagues from the Reagan administration, former assistant secretary of defense Richard Armitage and former chief of staff Kenneth Duberstein. The four discussed pros and cons and brainstormed over many days. Powell was leaning toward running for president, and he was telling the Draft Powell committees to keep up the good work.

Powell wavered back and forth during these discussions, and he was on an emotional roller coaster. Son Michael described what people expected of Colin Powell as president:

> One person is supposed to heal 200 years of racial divide. You're supposed to moderate the Republican party. You're supposed to create a foreign policy in a vacuum left by the Cold War. Solve Bosnia and lead us to a new era of prosperity and growth. All because you were a successful general and won a war.[14]

In the final meetings, Armitage noted that Alma Powell was opposed to the run for the presidency. Her opposition was "deep, heartfelt, immutable."[15]

The announcement was scheduled in a hotel ballroom in Alexandria, Virginia, on November 9, 1995. "Such a life requires a calling that I do not yet hear," Colin Powell said. "And for me to pretend otherwise would not be honest to myself, it would not be honest to the American people. And therefore I cannot go forward."[16] Supporter Charles Kelly who had headed up one of the Draft Powell committees summed it up for many disappointed supporters. "It's a sad day for us and a sad day for the country."[17]

So where does Colin Powell go from here? He has joined the Republican party, and in February 1996, he joined with others in the party to honor former President Ronald Reagan on his eighty-fifth birthday. When asked about the vice presidency, Powell ruled it out. He said he would devote his time to educational and charitable works.

Michael Powell says:

> I wouldn't be surprised one bit if he was in government again as secretary of something, or even

Only time will tell what future role Colin Powell will play in United States history.

Vice President. And I'm not entirely convinced he wouldn't run [for president] in 2000. He's only 58. In 2000 he'll be 10 years younger than Dole will be in 1996.[18]

Colin Powell has already lived a remarkable life. Only time will tell what future role he will play in a country he obviously loves profoundly.

CHRONOLOGY

1937—Born in Harlem, New York, on April 5.

1958—Graduates from City College of New York as ROTC Distinguished Military Graduate.

1959—First Army tour of duty—Fulda Gap, Germany; becomes platoon leader of forty men; promoted to first lieutenant.

1962—Marries Alma Johnson in Birmingham, Alabama; promoted to captain.

1963—First tour of duty in Vietnam; Michael Powell, first child, is born; injured by enemy booby trap in July.

1965—Second child, Linda, is born.

1966—Promoted to major.

1968—Second tour of duty in Vietnam; involved in rescue of comrades after helicopter crash; receives Soldier's Medal for bravery.

1969—Returns to Washington, D.C., to attend master's degree program at George Washington University.

1970—Promoted to lieutenant colonel; third child, Annemarie, is born.

1972—Becomes White House Fellow working at the Office of Management and Budget in Washington, D.C.

1973—Tour of duty in Korea.

1976—Promoted to colonel.

1979—Promoted to brigadier general.

1982—Command at Fort Leavenworth, Kansas; develops project to honor the buffalo soldiers.

1983—Promoted to major general; military assistant to Secretary of Defense Caspar Weinberger.

1986—Promoted to lieutenant general; commander of V Corps in Frankfurt, Germany.

1987—Deputy to National Security Advisor Frank Carlucci in Washington, D.C.; becomes national security advisor.

1989—Promoted to full general; becomes Chairman of the Joint Chiefs of Staff; manages Operation Just Cause in Panama.

1990—Manages Operation Desert Shield.

1991—Manages Operation Desert Storm; in January is appointed to second term as Chairman of the Joint Chiefs of Staff.

1993—Retires as Chairman of the Joint Chiefs of Staff and from the Army.

1994—Forms part of an American delegation to restore elected government to Haiti.

1995—First book, autobiography, *My American Journey*, is published; considers run for presidency in 1996 but decides against it in November.

CHAPTER NOTES

Chapter 1

1. Howard Means, *Colin Powell: Soldier-Statesman—Statesman-Soldier* (New York: Fine, 1992), p. 156.

2. David Roth, *Sacred Honor: Colin Powell* (Grand Rapids, Mich.: Zondervan, 1993), p. 87.

3. Colin Powell, *My American Journey* (New York: Random House, 1995), p. 139.

4. Roth, p. 88.

5. Joe Klein, "Can Colin Powell Save America?" *Newsweek*, October 10, 1994, p. 26.

6. Means, p. 326.

7. Ibid., p. 20.

Chapter 2

1. Howard Means, *Colin Powell: Soldier-Statesman—Statesman-Soldier* (New York: Fine, 1992), p. 29.

2. Ibid., p. 30.

3. Colin Powell, *My American Journey* (New York: Random House, 1995), p. 239.

4. David Roth, *Sacred Honor: Colin Powell* (Grand Rapids, Mich.: Zondervan, 1993), p. 22.

5. Joe Klein, "Can Colin Powell Save America?" *Newsweek*, October 10, 1994, p. 26.

6. Means, p. 42.

7. Ibid., p. 44.

8. Powell, p. 12.

9. Ibid., p. 17.

10. Ibid.

11. Roth, p. 28.

12. Powell, p. 12.

13. Means, p. 50.

14. Ibid., p. 51.

15. Roth, p. 32.

16. Means, p. 53.

17. Roth, p. 32.

18. John Ranelagh, "American's Black Eisenhower," *National Review*, April 1, 1991, p. 26.

19. Klein, p. 26.

20. Laura B. Randolph, "General Colin L. Powell, the World's Most Powerful Soldier," *Ebony*, February 1990, p. 138.

21. Roth, p. 36.

22. Powell, p. 24.

23. Ibid., p. 25.

Chapter 3

1. Colin Powell, *My American Journey* (New York: Random House, 1995), p. 25.

2. Ibid.

3. David Roth, *Sacred Honor: Colin Powell* (Grand Rapids, Mich.: Zondervan, 1993), pp. 37–38.

4. Howard Means, *Colin Powell: Soldier-Statesman—Statesman-Soldier* (New York: Fine, 1992), p. 77.

5. Powell, p. 26.

6. Ibid.

7. Ibid., p. 28.

8. Ibid.

9. Ibid.

10. Colin L. Powell, "From CCNY to the White House," *City College Alumnus*, Fall 1988, p. 12.

11. Roth, p. 41.

12. Ibid., p. 42.

13. Ibid., p. 38.

14. Powell, p. 36.

15. Roth, p. 46.

16. Powell, p. 64.

17. Roth, p. 50.

18. Powell, p. 64.

19. Roth, p. 51.

20. Powell, p. 67.

21. Ibid., p. 66.

22. Ibid., p. 67.

Chapter 4

1. Colin Powell, *My American Journey* (New York: Random House, 1995), p. 68.

2. Howard Means, *Colin Powell: Soldier-Statesman—Statesman-Soldier* (New York: Fine, 1992), pp. 116–117.

3. Ibid., p. 118.

4. Ibid., p. 132.

5. David Roth, *Sacred Honor: Colin Powell* (Grand Rapids, Mich.: Zondervan, 1993), p. 58.

6. Ibid., p. 59.

7. Susan Watters, "The General's Lady," *Ebony*, September 1991, p. 56.

8. Powell, p. 87.

9. Roth, p. 65.

10. Ibid., p. 71.

11. Ibid., pp. 72–73.

12. Powell, p. 107.

13. Roth, p. 74.

14. Tom Mathews et al., "Nobody Knows My Politics," *Newsweek*, May 13, 1991, p. 21.

15. Roth, p. 73.

16. Roth, p. 74.

17. Means, p. 85.

18. Roth, p. 83.

19. Watters, p. 56.

20. Ibid., p. 55.

Chapter 5

1. David Roth, *Sacred Honor: Colin Powell* (Grand Rapids, Mich.: Zondervan, 1993), p. 95.

2. Caspar W. Weinberger, "General Colin Powell—An Inside View," *Forbes*, January 22, 1990, p. 31.

3. Roth, p. 98.

4. Howard Means, *Colin Powell: Soldier-Statesman—Statesman-Soldier* (New York: Fine, 1992), p. 181.

5. Carl T. Rowan, "Called To Service: The Colin Powell Story," *Readers Digest*, December 1989, p. 123.

6. Means, p. 181.

7. Roth, p. 100.

8. Ibid., p. 102.

9. Ibid., p. 103.

10. Ibid., p. 105.

11. Ibid., p. 107.

12. Cyrus Townsend Brady, *Indian Fights and Fighters* (New York: Doubleday, 1904), p. 354.

13. J. Norman Heard, *The Black Frontiersman* (New York: Day, 1969), p. 119.

14. Fairfax Downey, *Indian Fighting of the Army* (New York: Scribners, 1941), p. 25.

15. Means, p. 329.

Chapter 6

1. Howard Means, *Colin Powell: Soldier-Statesman—Statesman-Soldier* (New York: Fine, 1992), p. 211.

2. Ibid., p. 213.

3. Ibid., pp. 213–214.

4. Ibid., p. 218.

5. Ibid., p. 225.

6. Ibid., p. 247.

7. Colin Powell, *My American Journey* (New York: Random House, 1995), p. 343.

8. Laura B. Randolph, "The World's Most Powerful Soldier," *Ebony,* February 1990, p. 140.

9. Carl T. Rowan, "Called to Service: The Colin Powell Story," *Readers Digest,* December 1989, p. 124.

10. David Roth, *Sacred Honor: Colin Powell* (Grand Rapids, Mich.: Zondervan, 1993), p. 122.

11. Ibid., p. 123.

12. Rowan, p. 124.

13. Roth, p. 127.

14. Ibid.

15. John Ranelagh, "America's Black Eisenhower," *National Review,* April 1, 1991, p. 28.

16. Ibid.

17. *CBS Evening News,* May 16, 1995.

Chapter 7

1. David Roth, *Sacred Honor: Colin Powell* (Grand Rapids, Mich.: Zondervan Publishing House, 1993), p. 131.

2. Colin Powell, *My American Journey* (New York: Random House, 1995), p. 401.

3. Bob Woodward, *The Commanders* (New York: Simon & Schuster, 1991), p. 106.

4. Ibid.

5. Powell, p. 448.

6. Woodward, p. 106.

7. Means, p. 185.

8. John Ranelagh, "America's Black Eisenhower," *National Review,* April 1, 1991, p. 28.

9. Laura B. Randolph, "The World's Most Powerful Soldier," *Ebony,* February 1990, p. 138.

10. Roth, p. 163.

11. Ibid., p. 167.

12. Ibid., p. 168.

13. Ibid., p. 169.

14. Ibid., p. 159.

15. Ibid., p. 132.

16. Ibid., p. 134.

17. Ibid., p. 135.

18. Susan Watters, "The General's Lady," *Ebony,* September 1991, p. 56.

19. Ibid.

20. Randolph, p. 140.

21. Ibid., p. 138.

Chapter 8

1. Colin Powell, *My American Journey* (New York: Random House, 1995), p. 418.

2. Bob Woodward, *The Commanders* (New York: Simon & Schuster, 1991), p. 149.

3. Ibid., p. 153.

4. Ibid., p. 169.

5. Nathan A. Haverstock, "Panama," *The World Book Year Book* (Chicago: World Book, 1990), p. 404.

6. Powell, p. 464.

7. Tom Mathews, et al. "The Reluctant Warrior," *Newsweek,* May 13, 1991, p. 18.

8. Woodward, p. 260.

9. Ibid., p. 277.

10. Powell, p. 467.

11. General H. Norman Schwarzkopf, *It Doesn't Take a Hero* (New York: Bantam Books, 1992) p. 367.

12. Woodward, p. 320.

13. Schwarzkopf, p. 409.

14. Ibid., p. 373.

15. Michael Grant, "The Gulf War," *The San Diego Union Tribune,* March 10, 1991, p. C5.

16. Powell, p. 527.

17. John Ranelagh, "America's Black Eisenhower," *National Review,* April 1, 1991, p. 27.

Chapter 9

1. David Roth, *Sacred Honor: Colin Powell* (Grand Rapids, Mich.: Zondervan, 1993), p. 242.

2. Colin Powell, *My American Journey* (New York: Random House, 1995), p. 571.

3. Joe Klein, "Can Colin Powell Save America?" *Newsweek,* October 10, 1994, p. 26.

4. Howard Means, *Colin Powell: Soldier-Statesman—Statesman-Soldier* (New York: Fine, 1992), pp. 315–316.

5. Bruce W. Nelan, "Road to Haiti," *Time,* October 3, 1994, p. 36.

6. Ibid.

7. Ibid., p. 37.

8. Klein, p. 20.

9. Ibid.

10. George J. Church, "What Would Make Colin Powell Run?" *Time,* October 3, 1994, p. 37.

11. Means, p. 332.

12. Caspar W. Weinberger, "General Colin Powell—An Inside View," *Forbes,* January 22, 1990, p. 31.

13. John F. Stacks, "The Powell Factor," *Time,* July 10, 1995, p. 25.

14. Ibid., p. 26.

15. Ibid.

16. J.F.O. McAllister, "The Candidate of Dreams," *Time,* March 13, 1995, p. 88.

17. Means, p. 324.

18. Mark Z. Barabak, "Powell Keeping Cagy About Political Plans," *The San Diego Union Tribune,* May 21, 1995, p. A8.

Chapter 10

1. David Roth, *Sacred Honor: Colin Powell* (Grand Rapids, Mich.: Zondervan, 1993), p. 223.

2. Mark Z. Barabak, "Powell Keeping Cagy About Political Plans," *The San Diego Union Tribune,* May 21, 1995, p. A8.

3. Colin L. Powell, "From CCNY to the White House," *City College Alumnus*, Fall 1988, p. 13.

4. Clarence Page, "Conservatives and Colin Powell," *The San Diego Union Tribune*, July 14, 1995, p. B6.

5. Ibid.

6. Letter of Russell L. Adams, September 20, 1995.

7. *New York Times* News Service, "Powell Leery on School Prayer," *The San Diego Union Tribune*, September 12, 1995, p. A15.

8. Michael Kramer, "Just Like Ike," *Time*, September 18, 1995, p. 74.

9. John F. Stacks, et al. "I've Got to Make Some Choices," *Time*, September 18, 1995, p. 73.

10. Nancy Gibbs, "General Letdown," *Time*, November 20, 1995, p. 50.

11. Ibid.

12. Ibid.

13. Ibid., p. 51.

14. Ibid., p. 56.

15. Ibid.

16. Mark Z. Barabak, "I Cannot Go Forward," *The San Diego Union Tribune*, November 6, 1995, p. A1.

17. Ibid., p. A27.

18. Gibbs, p. 57.

FURTHER READING

Gibbs, Nancy. "General Letdown." *Time,* November 20, 1995, 54–56.

Heard, J. Norman. *The Black Frontiersman.* New York: Day, 1969.

Klein, Joe. "Can Colin Powell Save America?" *Newsweek,* October 10, 1994, 20–26.

Means, Howard. *Colin Powell: Soldier-Statesman— Statesman-Soldier.* New York: Fine, 1992.

Powell, Colin. *My American Journey.* New York: Random House, 1995.

Ranelagh, John. "America's Black Eisenhower." *National Review,* April 1, 1991, 26–27.

Roth, David. *Sacred Honor: Colin Powell.* Grand Rapids, Mich.: Zondervan, 1993.

Schwarzkopf, Gen. H. Norman. *It Doesn't Take a Hero.* New York: Bantam Books, 1992.

Stacks, John F. "The Powell Factor." *Time,* July 10, 1995, 24–29.

Woodward, Bob. *The Commanders.* New York: Simon & Schuster, 1991.

INDEX

MLK